7 Keys to Intimacy with Jesus

Matthew Robert Payne

Copyright © 2016. All rights reserved.

No part of this publication may be reproduced, stored in a retrieval system or transmitted in any way by any means, electronic, mechanical, photocopy, recording or otherwise, without the prior permission of the author except as provided by USA copyright law.

All scripture is taken from the New King James Version (NKJV) unless otherwise indicated. Copyright © 1982 by Thomas Nelson, Inc. Used by permission. All rights reserved.

New Living Translation (NLT), copyright © 1996, 2004, 2015 by Tyndale House Foundation. Used by permission of Tyndale House Publishers Inc., Carol Stream, Illinois 60188. All rights reserved.

Cover design: Akira007 from Fiverr.com

Editing by Lisa Thompson at writebylisa.com

The opinions expressed by the author are not necessarily those of Revival Waves of Glory Books & Publishing.

Published by Revival Waves of Glory Books & Publishing
PO Box 596| Litchfield, Illinois 62056 USA
www.revivalwavesofgloryministries.com

Revival Waves of Glory Books & Publishing is committed to excellence in the publishing industry.

Book design Copyright © 2016 by Revival Waves of Glory Books & Publishing. All rights reserved.

Published in the United States of America

Paperback: 978-1-68411-086-5

Hardcover: 978-1-68411-087-2

Dedication

My Cat

I dedicate this to my cat, Scampie, that died when I was 8 years of age. Your loss in my life caused me to embrace Jesus as my friend. I know that you can read this as I type, and I know that you are waiting for me in heaven. I have never dedicated one of my books to you, but without you dying, I never would have met my best friend, Jesus.

May you watch all that I do, and may you pray for me, and may my life make you proud. See you soon!

Acknowledgements

Holy Spirit

I would like to thank the Holy Spirit for giving me the words to speak in this book. I want to thank him for being the conduit all these years to bring the voice of Jesus and the Father to me.

Jesus

Thanks for being my personal Friend and for being with me through everything — good and bad times alike.

Father

Thank you for loving me and having patience and grace for me.

Lisa Thompson

Thank you for editing my words and polishing what I have written to make sure that this was a quality book.

Revival Waves of Glory Books and Publishing

I want to thank Bill Vincent, the head of this publishing company, for making this book available on Kindle and paperback and eventually, Audible. Bill does a terrific job.

Akira007 from Fiverr.com

I want to thank my graphic artist who designed the cover for me.

Enemies

I want to thank all of the people who have made my life hard and who have attacked me and tried to bring me down. Your sustained attacks gave me the desire to draw so close to Jesus. I pray for you all.

Readers of this Book

I want to thank everyone who has downloaded this book from Kindle. I write for you, and without you, I would have nothing to say. Thank you for letting me speak from my heart to you. I appreciate your support.

Table of Contents

Dedication i

Acknowledgements iii

Introduction 1

Key 1 – Obedience 2

Key 2 – Prayer 15

Key 3 – Asking Questions 28

Key 4 – Right Theology 39

Key 5 – Being Set Apart 51

Key 6 – Word of God 62

Key 7 – Friendships 76

Closing Thoughts 87

I'd love to hear from you 88

How to Sponsor a Book Project 99

Other books by Matthew Robert Payne 90

About the Author 92

Introduction

The journey from a normal relationship with Jesus that starts with being born again to a tremendously intimate relationship with him can be a long one. You cannot shortcut intimacy or simply read a book about it and be magically connected with Jesus.

Like anything worthwhile, a great friendship and relationship with Jesus takes time and effort. In this book, I share seven keys that are important to me and that have worked for me. I rarely find a person who has a closer relationship with Jesus. In my time, I have met a lot of Christians.

Without boring you too much, I will delve into the keys by using my own life and own stories to illustrate the points that I am making. I have presented the book as the Holy Spirit directed me about what to speak in the seven, 30-minute videos that were the first draft of the book. It is my prayer that you will not only read this book and apply these keys but that you will put the work into developing your own intimate relationship with the King of Kings.

Key 1 — Obedience

Many people might want to pursue intimacy with Jesus. I have a very intimate relationship with him.

Some people that know me have a sort of holy jealousy of my relationship with Jesus. They are jealous of the following:

- Jesus talks to me.
- He appears to me.
- I've been to heaven many times.
- He sends saints down to talk to me.
- I see angels.

Many factors contribute to a real, holistic relationship with Jesus.

Jesus wants to be your friend. Just like a husband or a wife, you spend a lot of time with this person and interact with them. They're involved with every major decision in your life. They give you advice and counsel. They're there in the good times and in the bad. Just like a husband or a wife, Jesus wants to be there for you.

He wants to be the person that helps you make decisions. He wants to be consulted as you walk through life. He actually wants to lead you. He truly wants to tell you each step to take and to guide and direct your path.

Psalm 37:23 puts it this way: *"The steps of a good man are ordered by the Lord, And He delights in his way."* That's true of Jesus.

The first subject we're going talk about is obedience. I want to share a Scripture with you that is very special to me, a very integral and a cornerstone of my relationship with Jesus. It's found in John 14:21 and says: *"He that has My commandments and keeps them, is he who loves Me. And he who loves Me will be loved by My Father and I will love him and manifest Myself to him."*

There's so much depth in that passage. Jesus is speaking, and he says, "He that has My commandments and keeps them, is he who loves Me."

First of all, most Christians have no idea that Jesus has over 50 commandments in the Bible, 50 things that he said to do and not to do. I'd estimate that more than 80 percent of Christians don't know that he gave 50 commandments.

Please note that it says, "He who has my commandments and keeps them." How can you keep his commandments if you don't know what they are?

The person who has his commandments and keeps them is a person who loves him. He's saying that people who don't have his commandments don't really love him.

People are sometimes surprised to know that he gave 50 commandments. In the Kindle book, I'll provide a link where you can read all of them. I wrote this article some years ago, and you can find it through Google if you are reading the paperback. It's called "The Fifty Commands of Jesus" at Ezine articles.

E-readers can follow this link: http://ezinearticles.com/?The-Fifty-Commands-of-Jesus&id=468177

Again, this verse is so important. Jesus says, "He that has My commandments and keeps them, is he who loves Me. And he who loves Me will be loved by My Father and I will love him and **manifest Myself to him**."

Jesus can manifest himself to you in two different ways.

As you know, the first way that he manifests himself is through his commandments. As you start to obey them through the help of the Holy Spirit, you start to develop the character of Jesus. You start to develop the mind of Jesus Christ.

The more you act like Jesus, the more you react and make decisions based on what Jesus taught, the more you will become like him and the more his character will manifest in your life.

Most people don't trust Jesus because they don't know him. Most people don't know him because they don't obey him.

When they obey him, they find out that he's smart and that his way is best; then they begin to trust him. The more they trust him, the more they can love him.

This develops as a continuing cycle, but it starts with obeying. It starts with knowing what he taught and obeying what he said.

Jesus Manifests Himself – Developing Character

This is the first type of manifestation that the verse speaks of. It means that you start to develop the character of Jesus Christ and to have his mind. You start to walk in the way that Jesus Christ taught and how he determined that we would walk.

I have never heard the following Scripture preached in church.

1 John 2:4, *"He who says 'I know Him' and does not keep His commandments is a liar, and the truth is not in him."*

John tells us here that if you say you know Jesus and you don't obey his commandments, then you're a liar.

Verse 5 follows: "But whoever keeps His word, truly the love of God is perfected in him. By this we know that we are in Him. He who says he abides in Him, ought himself to walk just as He walked."

John is saying here that the person who says he abides in Jesus ought to walk just as Jesus walked.

The Bible lists several verses chronologically that tell us that you need to obey Jesus and his commandments.

If you're obeying his commandments, then the love of God is perfected in you. Of course, this is because you live and walk in the commandments of Jesus. All of those commandments are an expression of love towards God and towards your neighbor.

You need to walk in love towards people. The more you walk in Jesus' commandments, the closer you grow to him. And the closer you are to Jesus, the more you can start to walk just like he walked.

Jesus didn't ever sin against anyone. We should be able to live that way, too. John compels us to live accordingly by what he wrote:

John 14:23 says, *"Jesus answered and said to him, 'If anyone loves Me, he will keep My word, and My Father will love him and we will come to him and make our home with him. He who does not love Me does not keep My words. And the words which you hear are not mine but the Father who sent Me.' "*

Jesus is saying here, "If you love me, keep my commandments." In fact, Jesus told the disciples, "If you love me, keep my commandments," four times between the Last Supper and his crucifixion.

Once again, just before he ascended, he commanded the disciples to teach everyone all that he taught them. That was the fifth time he mentioned obeying his commandments. We can see how important this is to him because of the repeated emphasis he placed on it.

Jesus Manifests Himself – Jesus Shows Up

The second understanding of "I will manifest myself to him," is when Jesus actually turns up.

Again, to emphasize this point, John 14:23 says, *"If anyone loves me, he will keep my word and My Father will love him, and we **will come to him** and make our home with him."*

This verse isn't just talking about the Holy Spirit. While Jesus talked about the Holy Spirit in this chapter, God the Father and Jesus are turning up in your house. They are manifesting themselves in visions and meeting with you and spending time with you in the same way that they have done in my life.

Jesus has turned up many times in my house, but God the Father has shown up a couple of times, too. It's a wonderful feeling — sitting down and conversing with God and Jesus. This is a tremendous relationship to have.

In the year 2000, 16 years ago, I met a group called the "Jesus Christians" who were all about practicing what Jesus taught. At that time, they had a collection called "the Top 40" in a tract. They spelled out the 40 commands of Jesus and what they actually meant. They had a little description about what it meant to keep each one of the commands.

I gave this list to my mother and asked her to go through the Gospels and add to the list, and she came up with a total of 50 commands.

I wrote an article with the 50 commands and the Scripture references for them. I couldn't remember all 50 of the commands. However, I remembered a few of them, and I started to practice those.

One of the commands that I remembered was that Jesus said to *"Give to everybody who asks of you"* (Luke 6:30). I put that into practice. Every time a beggar asked me for money, I gave him what I had — $2 here, $1 here, $5 there. I simply gave according to what I had and what I felt led by the Lord to give to the people. I just started giving and gave away thousands of dollars that way over the years. Giving really enriched my life.

Jesus started to turn up in my life. My life became a whole lot more intimate as I obeyed Jesus Christ just in simply obeying that command. Jesus taught many things. We grow closer and closer to him by obeying him and what he taught.

Examples of Obedience

I just want to share a few stories about obedience. Around that time, I was walking through my city down near the harbor where the ferries come in and the ships dock.

Everyone was outside this bar, and about 100 people were watching the Olympics on these big television screens. People were not even chatting but just standing at this outside bar.

Jesus told me, "Tell these people that the Olympics is a form of idolatry. It's okay to watch the Olympians, but they should recognize that all the Olympians were born with gifts and talents. The true person they should be glorifying is Jesus Christ who created them."

I asked Jesus, "When do you want me to say that?"

He replied, "Say it now."

That was very hard to do. I shouted out that message to the people, told them that watching Olympics is idolatry and added that they should respect and give honor to their Creator. Every time they see someone set a new world record, they should realize that God the Creator allowed them to be so fast and allowed them to perform so well.

Everyone turned their eyes from the screen and listened to me. I went on for about 30 seconds to a minute, and then, I stopped and walked away. That's obedience!

Now, I'm a prophet, and sometimes, I'm called to do radical things. The prophets in the Bible did some weird things. One of them had to walk naked around Jerusalem for a year as a sign and message. Today, he'd be arrested, but back then, he wasn't.

Another prophet had to cook his food on cow dung and just lay on his side for a certain amount of days and then lay on his other side for a certain amount of days. They were doing prophetic acts.

That shouting out I did about the Olympics might have affected maybe five people out of that hundred. But Jesus had at least one person in that group that he wanted to impact.

After I shared the message with the people, I caught a ferry to a beach in Sydney. I was with a friend who was a New Zealander. He met another New Zealander on the other side at the beach and started talking. They rubbed noses together as is the custom of two islanders.

Suddenly, I was hit by this massive wave of peace. It was so strong that I had to sit down. It was just an overwhelming feeling of peace, and my whole body went numb. I was so full of peace and joy, which was amazing.

I asked Jesus, "What is this?"

He answered, "This is my peace. This is my reward for what you did for me."

I was really impressed with the peace and the feeling that I had, which lasted for about five minutes.

My friend talked to the person he met. When they finished, the peace had subsided, and I was able to get up and continue my walk to the beach. We had a couple of beers at the pub, and I had a nice meal for dinner and then came home on the ferry. That's one example of obedience.

The second thing I want to talk about, which I illustrated, is that you have the ability to hear from Jesus. About 80 percent of Christians don't know how to hear from Jesus as a quiet, still, inner voice, which is a shame. However, you can be taught.

When you hear from Jesus, you step up to another level of obedience. You are compelled to obey the commands of Jesus when you know them, but Jesus or the Holy Spirit tells you to do specific things from time to time.

When you hear from Jesus, you need to obey his verbal commands. When he tells you to do something, obey what he tells you to do.

I was talking to Jesus once, and he asked me, "Do you know why most people don't hear from me?"

I told him, "I didn't really want to know," because it sounded like a negative answer.

He replied, "Do you know why they can't hear from me and why they don't want to hear from me?"

I answered, "I can't imagine why."

He stated, "They're afraid that if they hear from me, they'll have to do what I tell them to do. They are afraid I'm going to tell them to do something that they don't want to do. Instead, they just play church and religion. They go to church once a week and go to Bible study, but they don't lend their ear to me to hear what I'm saying because they're afraid of what I'm going to say."

Jesus might call you to shout out to people watching the Olympics and tell them it is idolatry.

You have to consider that I've been walking with the Lord and hearing from him for many years. As such, the Lord progressively gives instructions that might become harder. He won't ask all of you to do the same things that he asks me to do. A person grows in his obedience.

For many years, I went to the movies once every two weeks when I got my pension. Even when I was working at jobs, I used to go to the movies once every one or two weeks, depending on how often a good film came out.

At one stage in my life, years ago, Jesus told me that I wasn't to go to the movies anymore. I was saddened by that. That's the sort of thing you'd question to see if you're actually hearing from Jesus when you hear something that you don't want to hear.

At that time, I went to the movies to process my pain. I'd pick dramatic films that I knew would make me cry. I was able to offload my pain and suffering every two weeks and have a good cry and release tensions and sadness during the films. That was my way of self-medicating.

Jesus decided that instead of crying at the movies, he wanted me to come to him. He wanted me to release my pain to him and the Father in a better and more therapeutic and holistic way instead of releasing my pain at the movies.

I went for over a year without going to the movies. One day, I was walking along the main street of our city, opposite the cinemas. A film was playing called "Cinderella Man" with Russell Crowe.

Jesus told me, "You can go and see that movie tonight." I went across to the movies and found out when it was going to start. I ate dinner at McDonald's, and half an hour later, I was sitting in the movie for the first time in over a year. I cried my eyes out during that inspirational film. I've actually seen that movie five times now.

Jesus told me that I could go start going to the movies again after I saw that movie.

At the time, when Jesus told me I couldn't watch movies anymore, it was my only joy in life. I was in a pretty sad and depressed state. The only enjoyment I really had, and the only thing I really liked to do was to go to the movies once every one or two weeks.

When Jesus told me to give that up, I felt like I was giving up my only joy. I learned the sweet but bitter taste of obedience and learned that Jesus had his reasons for why he wanted me to give up movies. It was bittersweet because it really hurt. It was really hard to do, and it was an activity that I truly loved.

Jesus wanted to know that I could put this activity on the altar and obey him and give it away.

This was one of the toughest tests of my life. Every time a movie was advertised on TV that sounded like it was going to be a good movie, I cried in my heart. All that year, movies came out that I couldn't see. I still watched TV, but I didn't go to the movies.

You grow close to Jesus by doing each thing that he commands you to do or that he leads you to do. Over time, you grow closer and closer to him.

I can't stress enough how important obedience is. Like Jesus told me, many people don't hear from him because they're afraid that he will tell them to do something that they don't want to do.

There's a lot of truth in that.

If you can't hear from Jesus now, I encourage you to find a book on how to hear from him and learn what to do. I encourage you to read my article on the 50 commands of Jesus and start to put them into practice.

You'll see your relationship with Jesus start to change. Not only will he start to manifest his personality in your life, not only will you start to develop the mind of Christ, but as you obey each of his commands, your life will become more rewarding.

It's no small thing to have the character of Jesus, but it's something to be prized. Many people will see you when you're out and about and doing life with people. They will see your character and see how kind you are.

I've got a third story here that I want to share with you. Last week, I asked the members in one of the Facebook groups that I run to share how God has worked in their lives.

This woman posted. She stated that she was at the church and a man that raped her came to church. It was the second time he came to church. He didn't recognize her, but she recognized him as her rapist.

Jesus told her, "I want you to go and ask him what his needs are." She admitted that it took her the whole service to find the grace and the courage to walk up to him and ask him about his needs.

As he started talking, he began to cry. He told her that his father was dying. His father didn't know the Lord, and he was afraid that his father was going to go to hell.

She felt the need to do more than pray for him. She actually went back to his father's bedside and shared the Gospel with the father and led him to the Lord. Two hours after she left the hospital, the man passed away.

This is just a radical encounter with the Spirit of the Lord and being led by the Spirit of the Lord. Her rapist's father is now going to heaven because of her act of obedience.

If she hadn't acted, that father would have been in hell. If she had not forgiven her rapist and not been used to pour out love on her rapist, that man would have spent an eternity without Jesus.

I do not share this story to justify rape or what happened to that woman in any way. However, this is an example of radical love — the love that Jesus has called us to. That's the sort of love that he wants to see us moving in.

I was compelled to share these three stories about obedience with you. I have to say that I do have a wonderful life with Jesus. He has manifested his character in my life and many people say that to me in personal prophecies.

He's also manifested himself in visions to me. He's also turned up in the flesh, and I have interacted with him as a human being. Obedience brings many joys.

Key 2 — Prayer

Many people consider going to church, praying and reading the Bible as essential foundations to the Christian faith, and that's been proven through time to be true. One of the keys to special intimacy with Jesus is to pray to the Lord. I'm a little different from many Christians that live, different in how I talk to Jesus and how he talks back and the conversations we have.

I rarely have a one-way prayer with Jesus when he doesn't talk back. Most of the time, we have conversations as if I were at a café, sitting and talking with a friend. When you go to a café with a friend, you don't talk for half an hour while your friend says nothing. Sure, you might go on for five minutes with a story, but then your friend comments and asks questions about it. It's very rare to sit down with a friend and talk for half an hour without your friend speaking.

In the same way, I have an interactive, two-way conversation with Jesus, and I encourage people to do the same. You can have a two-way conversational prayer with Jesus by keeping a journal and writing down your prayers and asking Jesus questions. He will give you the answers, and you can write what Jesus is saying to you in your journal. This is very handy when you come back to it and read it months or years later. You can read what Jesus was saying to you and see how you have grown and developed and how the things that he has said have come true in your life and how you've worked through things.

I've looked at journals that I wrote years ago, and it's very encouraging to see the growth that I've made since the time I wrote them. It lifts me up to hear what Jesus said to me and see that many things that he said would happen have come to pass.

I really suggest that people start to hear from Jesus and start to hear him speak by learning to journal and starting to write down your prayers. Record your prayers and listen to Jesus and ask him to address you by name and answer your questions. You can ask him questions and listen to his answers and write them down. You can even take your journal to a trusted friend or to your pastor and show him or her what you are hearing. Ask them to confirm that it really is Jesus so that you can be sure that he is speaking. This is an amazing way to start your prayer life and to hold an interactive, two-way conversational prayer with Jesus. It's very safe because you've written down what Jesus said, and you can show it to others and seek confirmations from them that Jesus was really talking to you.

I listen to Andrew Wommack. Once, he had a guest come and visit his ministry, and his guest asked him, "How long do you pray each day?"

Andrew replied, "I'm not going to answer that. Simply because if I pray more than you, you might feel embarrassed about that and upset that you don't pray as much as me. Yet if I say how long I pray, and you pray longer, and you tell me, then I might feel bad and upset with myself. So I just say that I pray as often as I need to."

Even so, the conversation sort of worried Andrew, and he was talking to the Lord, and the Lord spoke to him about it. Andrew's wife's name is Jamie.

The Lord told him, "If you had the choice of spending the whole day with Jamie doing errands and shopping and puttering around the house, doing house work or if you had the chance to go out to dinner with her for just an hour, spending one-on-one time, what would you choose to do?"

Andrew answered, "I would choose to spend the whole day with Jamie."

Jesus responded, "Then why do you limit time spent with me to one hour a day?"

This was really great insight to me. It was a very encouraging word when I heard that because I realize that each day, I'm being ministered to by the Holy Spirit. I spend each day in the presence of Jesus.

Paul was referring to this in 1 Thessalonians 5:17, *"Pray without ceasing."* This is a constant state of readiness toward the Lord. It's a state where each moment of the day, you're in communion with the Holy Spirit and Jesus. You can spend your time in his presence and ask Jesus questions as things come up during the day. You don't have to limit Jesus to your schedule of time in the morning and a few minutes at night. You can spend the whole day communing with Jesus and be in continued fellowship and prayer.

I wanted to share with you a few prayers that I've prayed in my life that impacted and really encouraged me. These stories show you that prayer works.

At 14 years of age, I was in a Baptist church with a pastor who was a very good communicator and preacher. He taught a series on different saints. One week, he preached a sermon on

Abraham, and he spoke about how Abraham left everything, including his family, his place of birth and his friends and left with just his wife and his sheep and his cattle. He started traveling to an unknown destination with the knowledge that God was going to share with him where to settle down.

Today, it would be really weird if someone moved from where they are to where God tells them to go without having a specific destination. It might be as if the Lord told them to buy an around-the-world airfare ticket and just go and visit different countries, and he'd tell them which country to settle in when they arrived.

Abraham not only moved when God told him, but he also took Isaac to the mountain to sacrifice him. Abraham did a lot of radical things, and it was certainly radical for him to prepare to kill his son who God had promised to build a nation from. I listened to the story of Abraham as a 14-year-old boy, and the pastor really explained it well. My pastor had shared that Abraham was called "a friend of God's."

I came home that day and knelt by my bed in my usual manner. I asked Jesus, "Could I be a friend of God like Abraham one day? Could people refer to me as a friend of God's? Could I be known that way?"

I've been involved in prophetic groups for a number of years and had hundreds of prophecies spoken over me in the last few years. I'm happy to say that a number of the prophecies have said that I'm like Abraham, a friend of God. It's now been 35 years since I prayed that prayer. I have experienced a lot of heartache, trials and turbulence in my life, but I've finally become a friend of God's. I'm a very close and intimate friend with Jesus, and I'm also a friend of God's. This was a prayer that I prayed with faith and innocence. I had no idea of the trouble that would come into my life when I prayed that prayer. But through all of it, I became a friend of God's.

Another prayer that I prayed was based on another sermon that my pastor preached the same year on David. He went through David's life and how he slaughtered Goliath and how he ran from Saul for many years. He shared how he waited for Saul to die, and then, he reigned as king. He reigned for a total of 40 years — 33 years in one place and seven years in Jerusalem. My pastor went on to share that David was a man after God's own heart.

I've come to establish that a man after God's own heart consists of two parts. First, this man wants God's own heart on things. He wants to have a heart like Solomon who can manage the people correctly and who needs God's heart and God's wisdom so that he can judge his people. A man after God's own heart is someone who wants to have the mind of God and the emotions of God so that he can make decisions and act accordingly. We're told in 1 Corinthians 2:16 that we have the mind of Christ.

In one way, David was a man after God's own heart. Secondly, David was also a person who pursued God with all that he had. He wanted to win the heart of God. This is probably the most commonly understood version of what it meant for David to be a man after God's own heart.

I went home as a 14-year-old boy and knelt by my bed and said, "I want to be like David, a man after your own heart, God." I have to confess that once again, after the last five years through prophetic circles and prophetic words, people have said that today, I'm like David, a man after God's own heart.

I knew I'd developed and become like David with a shepherd's heart. My heart was strengthened with these confirming prophecies that I was a friend of God's and to be referred to as David, a man after God's own heart. Those prayers at 14 years of age were solid, fashioning prayers that really took effect. God took notice of them and started the cogs moving for me to progress so that I would become the person that I am today.

Around the same age, I prayed another prayer. A man shared his testimony one night at church. He was covered in tattoos, and he told us that he was a biker. He had committed a lot of crimes and was addicted to heroin. He had slept with prostitutes and lived a very loose life. He was convicted of an offense and went to prison. While there, he was bored and read a Bible that was placed in the jail by the Gideon's organization and gave his life to Jesus. He spent the second half of his testimony talking about the Jesus that he had come to know.

I knew Jesus pretty well at 14. I had been talking to him for years, but this man knew so much about Jesus. He knew things that I never knew. He was talking about Jesus and sharing things that were just amazing, which really astounded me. A man that looked like this normally wouldn't be allowed in a pulpit.

I went home that day and told Jesus that I didn't want a normal Christian testimony. I wanted a story that would impact people and at the end of it, I wanted to be able to share things about Jesus, intimate things about him, that no one else knows. I want to be able to have a relationship with Jesus that draws people in.

Today, that prayer has been answered. Today, I have written two books with unknown revelations about the life of Jesus in them. They are called:

- "Finding Intimacy with Jesus Made Simple" and
- "Jesus Speaking Today."

Both of these books contain extra-biblical information about the life of Jesus and what he went through and what he suffered. They share how he lived and how he was feeling when he was on earth. Both of these books give tremendous insight into the life of Jesus. I have become that person who knows a lot about Jesus and who knows a lot about his life on earth. I know a lot about Jesus intimately as a friend who talks to him every day. That was a life-fashioning prayer.

Around about that time, another visiting speaker came to our church named Arthur Blessitt. He walked around the whole world carrying a cross. He walked into our city with the cross, and he met up with someone in our church who invited him to come and stay at their house. The person called the pastor, and the people of the church contacted others and arranged a meeting for Arthur to speak that night at our church.

We went to church to hear him speak. Years later, my mom remembered that his face shone with the glory of God. All I remember is that I was fascinated with this guy. As a young child, I wanted to be an evangelist, and I knew that he was an evangelist. He had a book with his life story, and I asked my mother to buy the book because I wanted to read it.

I bought the book, and I read a story in the book of when he was out walking, and Jesus appeared to him. He had a conversation with Jesus for about an hour. When he came home, he knocked on his door. He must not have had his key, so his wife opened the door. His wife observed, "You've seen Jesus," and she slammed the door on him. Apparently, his face was shining like the sunshine. He had so much glory from talking to Jesus, and he knocked on the door again and begged his wife to let him in.

I read that story and I prayed to Jesus, "I want to meet you." I was fortunate that I prayed all of these prayers as a young man of 14 before I'd grown to be an adult.

Since I prayed that prayer, I have seen Jesus and have been to heaven many times in visions. If people can handle it, I have even met Jesus in the flesh.

Prayer is a powerful thing. My growth into who I am and into what I have become these days is a result of prayer. I cannot stress how important prayer is for a close relationship with Jesus.

On another night in 2000, I was asleep. A lot of things happened during that year. Jesus talked to me in my dream and told me, "I want you to contact Jonathan Edwards." I knew that Jonathan Edwards was a medium who had a TV show in Australia for a year. I used to watch the TV show because I was fascinated with what he did.

I asked Jesus, "How do I do that?"

Jesus responded, "Just say his name."

So I said, "Jonathan Edwards," and this big shock wave of energy came through my head.

I heard Jonathan Edwards say, "This is Jonathan Edwards; who are you?"

I answered, "My name's Matthew Payne; I'm from Australia, and I'm living; I'm not dead."

He replied, "Yes, what's your message?"

I told him that Jesus doesn't want him to be a medium, and Jesus called him to other things. I told him that the Bible says that you shouldn't be a medium. I told him that his mother had raised him better than that. Then, I finished the message, and I woke up.

I normally take a couple of coffees to wake up, but that day, I was wide awake quickly.

Jesus told me, "He's trying to contact you again."

I asked, "What do I say?"

Jesus stated, "Don't worry; Michael, the archangel, is handling it from here."

Michael took over and must have said something more to him.

Jesus continued, "I want you to ask me for something now."

I commented, "What?"

Jesus stated, "When you pray, you never ask me for anything. Today, I want to reward you. I want to give you something, so ask me for something."

I questioned, "What should I ask you?"

He answered, "That's for you to decide."

About that time, I believe the Holy Spirit gave me a hint. I remembered the verse in Acts 2:17 that says, "Men shall dream dreams and sons and daughters shall prophesy."

I told Jesus, "I want prophetic dreams, and I want to have visions."

Just a few months later, I was coming home from my birthday celebration. I was walking home through a park and came to an intersection in the path. You have to take a left there, which meets at the center of the park, and then, you go a different direction. In the center of the park, I saw a vision of Jesus standing there with a couple of saints from heaven. This was the first time I saw Jesus in a vision.

Jesus greeted me, "Hello," and introduced the saints from heaven. One was Sadhu Sundar Singh. I think he died during the 1950s or 60s, and he was a famous apostle in India that I'd read about. Keith Green, the famous Christian singer, was there also. They both said hello and wished me a happy birthday. It was really exciting, especially because the first vision I had was on my birthday.

Since then, I've met Jesus many times. At one time, I was meeting Jesus in a vision every other day for a few weeks or so.

These are some of the prayers that I have prayed that Jesus has fulfilled in my life. I have prayed for other people many times.

On one occasion, a security guard that I knew at a Burger King approached me. I went there every Friday night after church. He asked me, "Can you pray for me?"

I answered, "What about? I don't really pray in public."

He stated, "Jesus told me to have you pray for me. You know, I really need your prayer."

I repeated, "What is it about?"

He informed me, "We have to move to another place in the city, and we need a five-bedroom house. I need God's provision; I need him to find us a house to rent. My daughter is going to university in another suburb, and we want to move so that she doesn't have to move out of our home."

I replied, "Ok, I'll pray." I prayed, "Dear Lord, open up a house for them, and when they see the house, make sure that no one else gets it but them. In Jesus' Name, I ask. Amen."

He came to me a couple of weeks later, and he told me they had the house and thanked me for my prayer. When he applied, he was interviewed, his application passed through, and they were happy to get the house. He reported that 126 people had applied for the house before he got it. God had answered my prayer and did not let anyone get the house except him.

One hundred and twenty-six people had tried to get that house, and God had put it together based on just the words of my prayer. I often pray for people and see results. An Indian apostle, Dr. D. G. Dhinakaran, in his book, "Gifts of the Holy Spirit," stated in his book that the prayers of a prophet are really powerful, and I agree (Word of Christ, publishing date unavailable).

I share these stories to show that one of the ways to intimacy with Jesus is to pray. Just as any relationship grows with time and conversations, so does your relationship with Jesus. When you have friendships that are real and solid, you have conversations with those people. Even with close friends on Facebook, you still use Facebook chat to talk to them, and you post things on their wall and communicate with each other. With friends that you know in your daily life, you spend time with them face to face and talk with them. How can we grow close to Jesus without spending hundreds of hours of talking to him and how can you know him intimately without a two-way conversation?

I encourage you to take the time to discipline yourself to get to know Jesus and learn how to hear his voice. I encourage you to buy yourself a journal and start to write down your prayers and journal and write down what Jesus has to say. Let Jesus speak to you through your journal each day. You don't need to spend more than 20 minutes, but what Jesus says is really precious, and it's great to have a record of his words.

I prayed and asked Jesus for things when I was young, and you have read about some of those prayers in this chapter and how they were fulfilled. When I learned to have two-way conversations with Jesus, I learned to simply chat with him, and my conversations hardly ever included me asking for anything. That's why Jesus told me to ask him for something when he answered my request for dreams and visions. I often spoke to Jesus, but I didn't ask for things.

Speaking to Jesus is an essential part of growing close to him. You can start with a journal to get used to hearing Jesus speak back to you, but soon enough, you will be ready just to have conversations with him. Jesus knows so much. He has so much wisdom. Jesus even knows who is going to be voted into power in any upcoming election.

I enjoy speaking to Jesus so much. He is a good friend to me, and he speaks really simply to me. He speaks in a down-to-earth manner as does God. I am about to publish a book called

"Conversations with God: Book 1." I find that God speaks simply to me. I find that both Jesus and God do not use big language with me that I can't understand, and they speak on my level. I am not trained theologically, and I am not very knowledgeable about fancy words in the English language, so they speak in a way that I can understand.

In this chapter, you have learned:

- The importance of journals
- The simple prayers of yours prayed with faith have a big impact and
- That you can chat with Jesus like a friend and not just have one-way conversations.

Key 3 — Asking Questions

I feel that this key is very important, and it has been an integral part of my relationship with Jesus. Of course, if you can't hear from Jesus or hear him speak, it would be hard to ask him questions and receive answers.

A friend of mine, Praying Medic, has released a book called "Hearing God's Voice Made Simple," (Inkity Press, 2015) which offers solid counsel to help you hear God speak. Another author, Adam Houge, has also written a number of books on hearing God speak. I learned to hear Jesus speak through the book, "Experiencing the Depths of Jesus Christ," by Madame Jeane Guyon (1648 – 1717).

How to hear from God is an essential part of a really rich relationship with Jesus Christ. One of the best parts of my life is having the ability to ask Jesus questions about certain things and hear his answers. It's one thing to read the Bible and understand what the Bible says about life and the Kingdom of God and the proper Christian life; it's quite another thing to interact with Jesus on a day-to-day basis and ask him questions and find the answers that he supplies that will custom fit like a glove. Jesus speaks firsthand about life and your specific situation. It's very handy to go through life and ask him questions about different aspects of your life and discuss what's important to you, even if it's not specifically in the Bible.

The Bible doesn't give us information about many things, such as what job to pick, what girlfriend to go out with and many other concerns. We need specific answers in our lives these days, and not everything is covered in the Bible. We are really fortunate to have a Savior, a God who is alive, a God that we can converse with and ask questions of and hear reliable answers that stimulate our minds and that direct us in the right course of action for our lives.

Jesus is only too willing to talk to us. He isn't a distant God; he is called "Emmanuel" in the Bible, which means "God with us." He wants to be next to us. He wants to be close to us. He wants to be a daily source of information for us; he doesn't want us to think of him as distant; he doesn't want us thinking that we're not able to approach him or ask him questions.

Like I stated in the previous chapter, it's one thing to pray, but it's quite another thing to have a two-way conversation or a relationship with Jesus. I shared in the last chapter that it's a good practice to buy a journal and write down your prayers to God. You can ask God or Jesus questions and then record their answers and what they say to you in a journal.

You can begin your journey of living life and leading a fulfilling and rich life through your Christian experience by recording the words of Jesus in a journal. You can not only hear what Jesus is saying as you record them; you can read them and reflect on the answers as time goes by and see your life take shape and happen according to what Jesus said.

I want to share some questions that I've asked Jesus in the rest of this chapter. These questions have come up in my life. Jesus was happy to answer them, so I've shared our conversations here.

I asked Jesus, "How do you cope with the current world?" We live in a world where many people are abused and suffering.

People are in forced slavery who make our chocolate and make our coffee. People in Japan and in China are doing very difficult work at really low labor rates with very long hours. So many people in this world are suffering.

I was interested in knowing how Jesus copes with that, so I asked him about it.

Jesus told me that he and his Father look forward to the future world where Jesus reigns.

I think that the future world and knowing what's going to happen keeps him happy. Of course, people might argue with that answer and say that Jesus is happy all of the time. But I just have to ask, "What sort of parent would be happy if their children were suffering, and if they couldn't do anything about it except to just stand back and watch?"

I'm aware that there may be people who really have no idea of the suffering in the world and of how that suffering pains Jesus and the Father and of how they weep for people who are hurting. It's understandable that people don't realize this.

I talked to him about this, and he's looking forward to the Christians in this world taking responsibility for these matters before he rules the world. He is looking forward to Christians exercising their dominion and their rightful status and their authority on the earth. He anticipates seeing revival break out and the Kingdom advance throughout the world. But he says that he and his Father cope by thinking of the future world.

I asked Jesus another question about his brother, James. I received insight from Jesus that his brother never really believed in him as the Messiah or as the spiritual leader. James didn't confess Jesus or believe in him as the Savior of the world until Jesus rose from the dead. Scripture mentions that Jesus appeared to James and the disciples in 1 Corinthians 15:7. James is mentioned by name because Jesus had a future for him and a reason to appear to him and show him that he really was beyond the grave and beyond death, and he was more powerful than his brother gave him credit for.

Jesus shared with me that James was especially cruel to him, picked on him, made fun of him and called him names. A typical sibling can treat us this way — cruel and unloving and unkind. Jesus was happy to say that his relationship with James transformed through the Holy Spirit during the few days that he was around after his resurrection and before his ascension. Jesus was able to develop a lasting relationship with James after he ascended.

It was really handy to find out information about James who went on to write the book of James. It was a revelation that James was one of Jesus' biggest critics. The Gospels tell us that Jesus couldn't perform many miracles in his hometown of Nazareth because of the unbelief of the people (Matthew 13:57, 58). This wore on Jesus' heart. Jesus further stated that a prophet is not without honor except in his home town and among his own family. Jesus said this because of how his family treated him. This was his experience; he was well-known and accepted and well-established among strangers and in other cities and places that he traveled. He was very popular, and people came from other nations to meet him and to hear him speak and to listen to him and to receive healing from him. But in his own hometown, he couldn't do many miracles and among his own family, he wasn't believed or seen as credible. It would have been hard to accept that your brother was going to save the world and lead Jews and establish a new faith. It's really interesting to talk to Jesus and question him about his life on earth, and I find out more information about what his life was like here.

I have two books that share more information about the life of Jesus in greater detail. "Finding Intimacy with Jesus Made Simple" tells all about Jesus' life on earth and how he was feeling. I also have a book called "Jesus Speaking Today" with 67 incidents of Jesus speaking. In the middle of each post or chapter, Jesus shares about his actual life as it relates to that topic. It's very insightful and full of revelation and wisdom, and you can really draw close to Jesus.

At one time, as I read the Bible, I finished all of Paul's letters, and I got to the end of Peter. 2 Peter 3:16 tells us that Paul's writings are hard to understand. The passage says that some people use and twist them to lead people astray. When I read that verse, I agreed with it, and I thought to myself that Paul was very hard to understand. I was upset because I was trying to learn about God and the Christian faith, but I came across someone who was hard to understand.

I agreed with Peter, and as I did, Jesus told me, "I want you to read my Gospels. As you read them, try and understand the situation that I was in at the time; try and understand the audience and what I was saying and what I meant when I said what I did. Try and understand how I was feeling in each of these situations." I obediently spent a number of years reading the Gospels and seeking Jesus for the understanding of his parables and what they meant specifically to the people that he was sharing them with. I spent many hours thinking about the parables and asking Jesus questions about them.

During this time, I was in McDonald's in Sydney. A homeless man appeared, and I was looking after him, spending time with him. I grew tired at one stage, so I told the homeless man that I was going to the toilet. On my way, I asked Jesus in my mind, "How long do I have to be with this homeless man?"

A song came on the radio and played with these words, "It ain't over 'til it's over."

I received that as the answer to the prayer that I had just prayed. I went into the toilet, splashed water on my face and refreshed myself and returned to spend more time with the homeless man.

I came back to him, and he announced clearly, "It's amazing, isn't it?"

I answered, "What is?"

And he replied, "When you ask Jesus a question, and he answers you with a song on the radio."

Right away, he had my attention and he continued, "Do you want me to share with you what I feel Jesus was teaching when he was on earth?"

Jesus had told me not to leave the Gospels or to read anywhere else so that was my mission at the time. I was very interested in hearing what this homeless man had to say. He started speaking, and each sentence was profound; it was truly rich and deep, so much so, that after one minute, my head was completely full, and I couldn't handle hearing any more information.

The only person that has previously impressed me like this has been Thomas Kempis in his writings, "The Imitation of Christ" (approximately 1420). He interviewed Christ, and Jesus responded with answers. Each page of that book is profound, but I had never heard such wisdom since that book. After a minute, I felt like asking the homeless man to please be quiet so that I could remember some of what he said. However, he was having such a fun time, and he had such a big smile on his face. It would've been very rude of me to tell him to be quiet.

Later, I was talking to another couple about the homeless man, and I told them, "I really think that it was Jesus in the flesh." I think that many people would have judged him by the way he looked even though he looked like the spitting image of the pictures of Jesus who just came out of Palestine. He was dressed in a white robe and had no shoes on.

I had many signs that day that I had met with Jesus. The final confirmation was when he disappeared into thin air later on, and I was assured that I had met Jesus.

After that experience, Jesus told me that if I had transcribed the words that the homeless man had spoken and printed them out, it would take 10 years to understand the depths of his words.

I would have never been able to understand this homeless man and captured the meaning of his words if I hadn't been obediently reading the Gospels like Jesus had asked. I have learned so much by reading the Gospels and asking Jesus questions.

I've received a lot of revelation on the teachings of Jesus, what he meant and how he felt when he was on earth. I learned these things from asking questions and from having a relationship with Jesus.

Either last year or the year before, I was seeing Jesus in visions every other day. One day, I was walking out of my place, and I normally saw Jesus' robe blowing in the wind, which meant that I was having a vision. I told Jesus, "I'm seeing you every second day now."

And Jesus responded, "I'm with you every day."

I asked him, "Where is that in Scripture?"

Jesus answered, *"And lo, I'm with you always, even to the end of the age* (Matthew 28:20)."

I said, "Granted."

Jesus answered, "I'm with you every day, Matthew. I am just choosing to manifest myself every second day." It profoundly affected me that Jesus really is always with us. He really is traveling beside us even if we are not aware of it and don't recognize his presence.

The Australian government ran a study inquiry into child sexual abuse, and information about it was playing on TV. Our prime minister, a female, had instigated it at the time. I asked Jesus, "What do you think of her?"

He answered, "I'm really proud of her and proud that she started this inquiry."

I asked, "What about the effect that all of these allegations are having on the church?"

Jesus replied, "Let the people of the church look after themselves. This is a time for the victims to have a voice and to share what they have been through and to find some sort of closure in their life."

Jesus was not taken by surprise about sexual abuse in a church or about how people in power misuse that power. This gave me insight into Jesus' heart as he really cared for the victims of child sexual abuse, and he really had a heart for them.

These are the types of questions that you can ask Jesus. Another time, I was meeting a friend of mine. We were in a food court in the city, and all of the saints in heaven were lining up to meet us. As each saint came to the table where we were, we'd hear the name of the saint, and I'd think of a question to ask them, and they would answer it.

Michael, the archangel, came front and center. I asked him, "Why is it getting so dark?"

He replied, "So that people like you will shine even brighter." His answer was remarkable. Some of the answers from Jesus are so real and so profound and so rich that you know that the answer was supernatural. You know that your own mind wasn't making it up.

So much of your Christian faith can be built up and encouraged by you thinking of questions and asking Jesus these particular questions about your faith and about the Bible. You can actually read the Bible and go through it and ask him questions about different verses in the Bible. As you're reading, you can hear a lot of running commentary from Jesus and the Holy Spirit. Jesus can be as real to you as a real friend.

He can be as present to you and as real to you as any friend that you have in life. He can actually be around you and manifest to you and show you that he's present more than a regular friend is in your life. He can have a richer experience with you than you can have with any friend. He's reliable, honest, trustworthy and faithful. Asking him questions will dig up things for you. Just like digging for buried treasure, you can ask Jesus question after question, and you develop a closer and closer relationship with him as you open up his resources, open up his mind and open up the depths of who he is to you.

You can only have an effect on people to the measure that you actually know Jesus. You can only have a positive Christian influence on people to the degree that you have intimacy with him.

Most of the people who are operating in powerful spiritual gifts and who have well-established ministries with a great effect on the world have an intimate relationship with Jesus. Intimacy with Jesus is built into their lives. I encourage you to get to know Jesus. Search out Praying Medic's book, "Hearing God's Voice Made Simple."

Read the book and do the exercises and practice so that you can learn to hear from Jesus. Then, take the time to question Jesus about specific things. Ask him what you want to know.

I'm quite confident that you'd have different questions than I do. Remarkably, we can connect with a man-God that is real, that is powerful and is ruling the universe with all the power that's been given to him. We can have him as our friend and our confidant. He can walk beside us and help us each day of our life and direct us and give us comfort and counsel. It's exciting to have such a man-God as part of our life. I encourage you to seek out Jesus and press in to hear his voice and grow in intimacy with him through asking him questions.

Key 4 — Right Theology

When you're seeking to draw close to Jesus, the theology that you hold and the ideas that you have about God and about Jesus play a very important role in your ability to draw close to them both.

Colossians 1:15, 16 says this, *"He is the image of the invisible God, the firstborn over all creation. For by Him all things were created that are in heaven and that are on earth, visible and invisible, whether thrones or dominions or principalities or powers. All things were created through Him and for Him."*

Jesus was the perfect image of the invisible God. 1 John 4:8 reminds us that, "He who does not love does not know God, for God is love."

We need to be reminded that God is a God of love and that Jesus is the Son of God. He is the exact image of the invisible God. When we look at the life of Jesus and what sort of person he was, that will encourage us to draw closer to Jesus.

We only have to look at how Jesus treated people when he was on earth to come to the realization that Jesus is a lot better than some people make him out to be. Some people have the mindset that Jesus went about rebuking the Pharisees all the time and causing trouble. They think that he was obstinate and against the religion of the day.

However, the Pharisees during those days were sent to investigate everyone who claimed to be the Messiah. Around this time, many people made these claims. This is similar to the investigations led by the Catholic Church into miracles and their declaration of people as saints when the miracles have been verified.

The Pharisees of that day had to check out the claims of people who said they were the Messiah, and they had to vigorously investigate people who were going around and collecting a following.

The Pharisees disproved these people, so they had an air of skepticism. Jesus was doing his best to respond, but they asked some unfair questions that came from a position of unbelief.

Jesus sometimes answered their questions with a question and avoided the original question that they had. Jesus often stood up to the Pharisees and stood his ground in the authority that he had.

However, when he was dealing with the common people, he was a person of love and compassion. The parable of the sheep and the goats (Matthew 25:31-46) explains this and proves what sort of person he was.

Jesus describes judgment day in the parable. He will say to those who are called to be sheep, *"I was hungry, and you fed me. I was homeless, and you took me in. I was in need of a drink, and you gave me something to drink. I was in the hospital, and you visited me. I was in prison, and you come to see me."*

That is typical of the love and the compassion of Jesus Christ. He modeled this behavior so that we would do the same. He calls us to be a friend of the hopeless and a friend of the broken-hearted, to build up the life of the downcast.

Jesus was aptly described in many places in the Bible. Isaiah 42:6-9 states the following: *"I, the Lord, have called You in righteousness, And will hold Your hand; I will keep You and give You as a covenant to the people, As a light to the Gentiles, To open blind eyes, To bring out prisoners from the prison, Those who sit in darkness from the prison house. I am the Lord, that is My name; And My glory I will not give to another, Nor My praise to carved images. Behold, the former things have come to pass, And new things I declare; Before they spring forth I tell you of them."*

"I, the Lord" means "I, the Father, God" "have called you," which is Jesus, "in righteousness." Jesus was sent as a light to the Gentiles to open blind eyes, to bring prisoners out of prison. Jesus was a remarkable person that came to bring a message of liberty and a message of grace to people that were bound up with laws and religion and all sorts of restrictions.

He was a demonstration of mercy and compassion to people who were broken, to people who were poor, to the people that were sad and to the people that didn't have any hope and certainly didn't have any way of coming to God outside of the strict religious system. They just didn't seem to be able to do everything — cross all the 't's' and dot the 'i's' — that the Pharisees and the teachers of the law demanded of them.

Jesus was a regular down-to-earth person who accepted people and who loved others and who demonstrated his love for people through the way he lived, talked and communicated with people.

This is the Jesus that we need to know. This is the Jesus who loves us that we need to understand. If we don't have a correct understanding of him, if we only see Jesus as the Jesus who leveled seven rebukes against the Pharisees and the Jesus that used whips in the temple, that will stop us from drawing close to him.

A wrong perception of who he is will keep us from him. We must do our research on Jesus, read the Gospels and understand the sort of person that he was.

Jesus got into trouble with the leaders of his day. You'll notice that he mixed with the publicans, the prostitutes and the sinners, so the Pharisees and the leaders of the law were quite outspoken when it came to Jesus. They asked him why he was hanging around the brokenhearted and the people who were obviously sinners.

The Pharisees were very strict. They are a lot like the people in churches today who can be very judgmental and legalistic and religious when it comes to people outside the church. They like to point fingers at people, including different people in the church.

On one hand, they expect perfection in people. On the other hand, they wear their own masks and the cloak of religion so that they appear to look bright and shiny to others.

But Jesus called out the leaders of his day, telling them that inside of themselves, they are dark and full of dead man's bones. Many of the words that Jesus used to address the Pharisees could be said today of certain elements of the church.

We must understand who Jesus is. We need to know that he was right and was a great teacher with unbelievable wisdom who understood the correct way to live in this world.

When he shared his parables and his commandments on how to live, we must understand that he is right. He is true; he is full of wisdom. To follow those commandments is the best practice for us as Christians.

John 14:21 tells us that if we truly love Jesus, we obey his commands. We can also spend time in prayer and talk to Jesus and develop an ability to have Jesus speak to us in conversations.

This will help you walk closer and closer with Jesus and develop your relationship in a sweet and intimate way. As we covered in key 3, you need to ask Jesus questions and to find words from him in Scripture and find the meaning of what is written in the Word and ask him specific questions about your life and theology.

We are covering theology in this section. For example, you might believe that God is a God of judgment. You might assume that Jesus is angry because he went through the temple to whip people. You might think he is angry because he rebuked the Pharisees. Jesus was very much against religion, and he is still against it today. You might focus on these actions and assume that he is angry and upset with the world in general.

You might focus on the anger of Jesus, which totally affects your ability to draw close to him. A fallen and angry father who abuses his children makes it hard for children to draw close to him and to trust him.

Similarly, you might not see Jesus in the correct light, and you might view him through the wrong theology and the wrong lens. This distorts your theology, leaving you with a wrong understanding and affecting your whole relationship with Jesus.

I speak from my own experience. For many years, I believed in an angry God who was a God of judgment who wanted a strict adherence to the law. He wanted us to be holy and pure and righteous.

I used to preach that way to people and come down hard on them. I did not encourage them and preached that the Christian life was a hard life. I preached the commandments of Jesus as a heavy burden of the law. I shared my views in a very religious way that wasn't loving. It wasn't caring. It wasn't compassionate toward anyone.

I was a hard task master. I was very religious and bound up in what I believed. I was a person that was sitting in the prison house of darkness, chained to my religion and chained to my beliefs.

I knew Jesus for many years, talked with him, had conversations with him and interacted with him. I had a relationship with him, but it wasn't as close as it could have been until I developed the right theology. My new theology said that Jesus is love; Jesus is caring; Jesus is understanding; Jesus is compassionate; Jesus forgives; Jesus loves, and Jesus will do anything to bring you into right relationship.

In fact, even when you sin, Jesus is there, waiting for you to turn around and embrace him. He told the story of the prodigal son who went away and lived a life of depravity and sin. But Jesus is like the father, and the father is like Jesus. The father in this story is waiting there, scanning the horizon for you to come back to him. Jesus and God want to run and embrace you. They don't even want to listen to the sins that you've committed and the excuses that you're giving and the promises that you have made.

The son came groveling home, begging to be a servant in his father's house. However, the father shut down what the son was saying, insisting, "Bring out the best robe and bring out some sandals and give him a signet ring." The father embraced him and threw a party to celebrate the prodigal. We might live a life of sin and condemnation. We walk in shame and guilt. We sin, so we think we're far from God.

Instead, Jesus died on the cross so that we could be found righteous and live a holy life. Although we fall from time to time, Jesus has made provision for us to be reconciled unto him and have a close relationship with him.

Anything short of understanding this will affect your ability to draw close to Jesus. Anything short of understanding your rights as a Christian and the true grace and understanding of Jesus and the true love that Jesus has and the way that the Kingdom properly works will limit your understanding and effectively cripple your ability to draw close to him.

I know what I'm talking about because I've lived that way myself. I lived a very religious life until I was illuminated to the message of grace. I understand the religious life. I understand living a life where you're angry, condemning and judgmental, and you don't have peace.

You might have this tremendous works mentality that says that you're not accepted by Jesus for being yourself. You're only accepted by what you do. In other words, you need to:

- Go to church
- Tithe
- Pray

- Read the Bible and
- Witness to people.

You might feel like grace plus works equals God's love. However, it's simply not true. I'll repeat myself. It's simply not true. Jesus loves people, and he loves them with an extraordinary love and a love that's full of compassion and understanding.

He wants people to worship him and draw close to him. He wants people to know him for who he is and not through the lens of wrong theology.

The Apostle Paul writes this in Romans 8:35-39, *"Who shall separate us from the love of Christ? Shall tribulation, or distress, or persecution, or famine, or nakedness, or peril, or sword? As it is written: 'For Your sake we are killed all day long; We are accounted as sheep for the slaughter.' Yet in all these things we are more than conquerors through Him who loved us. For I am persuaded that neither death nor life, nor angels nor principalities nor powers, nor things present nor things to come, nor height nor depth, nor any other created thing, shall be able to separate us from the love of God which is in Christ Jesus our Lord."*

That Scripture clearly says that nothing — **nothing** — can separate us from the love of God, his power and his ability to love us. Nothing can separate us from the love of Jesus.

This verse tells us quite clearly that we are wrong and mistaken if we think that our sins separate us from Jesus. We're wrong when we think that we have to live up to certain expectations or perform certain tasks to win the grace and favor of Jesus Christ.

Romans 8:1 says, *"There is therefore no condemnation for those who are in Christ Jesus who did not walk according to the flesh but according to the spirit."*

Jesus wants us to live our lives free from condemnation. Condemnation comes from the evil one, which he pours on us as he burdens us with feelings of guilt and shame that keep us separated from Jesus.

However, the Scripture above says, "nor angels nor principalities nor powers, nor things present nor things to come, nor height nor depth, nor any other created thing, shall be able to separate us."

Satan was created. Angels and fallen angels are created beings. None of those angels and principalities and powers — the hierarchy of demons — can separate us from the love of Jesus Christ. We need to understand that. We need to hold that dear.

If you don't understand these basic principles, you need to buy a copy of the book, "Destined to Reign," by Joseph Prince (Harrison House, 2010), which will show you some of the workings of grace and give you some understanding of grace because you need to come to know who Jesus is. You have to understand your rights and what it is to be loved by God. You need to see how hard and impossible it is to fall away from the love of God.

I heard a story of some Christians going to a bar. They mentioned Jesus to the bartender. She complained, "We won't have religion discussed in the bar, so please refrain from talking about that."

The man replied, "I'm not here to discuss religion with you. If I just mention the word Jesus, if I just mention his name, who do you consider that Jesus was? I'm not here to have an argument or to try and preach to you. I honestly want to know. Who do you consider that Jesus was?"

The woman relaxed and answered, "He is the most humble and beautiful man that walked the earth, full of love and compassion and understanding."

She was quite able to see the difference between religion and who Jesus was. The man that shared that story said that they started at that understanding and told her that they simply follow Jesus, and they want to demonstrate his love to the people in the bar.

Soon, the lady shouted that she was buying them drinks and brought them free food. Next, she introduced them to all her friends in the bar. They became part of that community. They regularly went back to that bar and fellowshipped with people, talking to people about real life encounters and situations, investing themselves in the lives of those people.

That's the sort of Jesus that people need to come to understand. They need to see that Jesus was a man of love, compassion, understanding, kindness and goodness.

We see the kind of love that Jesus had in 1 Corinthians 13:4-8, "Love suffers long and is kind; love does not envy; love does not parade itself, is not puffed up; does not behave rudely, does not seek its own, is not provoked, thinks no evil; does not rejoice in iniquity, but rejoices in the truth; bears all things, believes all things, hopes all things, endures all things. Love never fails."

That's the sort of love that Jesus demonstrates for us. He doesn't rejoice in iniquity. He isn't happy when we sin. Even so, he doesn't keep account of how many times we've sinned.

He bears all things, including our sin. He can handle it. He believes all things. He believes in our future. He endures all things.

His love never fails. His love doesn't run out. There's no end to his love. It's not as if you sin 300 times, but on sin number 301, you're crossed off Jesus' list, and he doesn't love you anymore.

He never stops loving you despite what you do and despite what you're doing. You don't have to jump through a bunch of hoops to satisfy Jesus.

You don't have to model your life after the perfect Christian in order to be accepted by Jesus. He loves you and accepts you just the way you are. He encourages you to walk with him, to get to know him, to place your trust in him, to communicate with him, to ask him questions, to grow in your understanding of him and in your understanding of the Father.

He wants to walk out that journey with you. He wants to fellowship with you. He wants to appear to you in visions and walk and talk with you. He wants to celebrate the good times in your life.

He wants to be with you through the hard times. He wants to be there when you need someone to lean on. He wants to be there when you need a friend to talk to.

He wants to be there when no one seems to understand you. He wants to be that friend that you have who is always there despite what happens. He doesn't want to be a fair-weather friend to you. He doesn't only love you when you're doing everything right. That's how the world loves, but he isn't like that.

Instead, he loves you and cares for you with a perfect love. He's drawing you through this book, and he's asked you to read this book. He's got messages in here for you. You can only understand him when you develop the right theology and the right understanding of who he is. You can do nothing to separate yourself from God.

Nothing can separate you from God through Christ Jesus. He wants you to know that you're loved; you're accepted, and you're beautiful. He loves every part of you.

Even in your mistakes, even in your weaknesses, he can find ways to work in your life and use you and demonstrate that his glory and his powers are flowing though you.

He wants to show you that, despite your failings, you can glorify him. Despite your weaknesses, you can be made strong through the power of his Holy Spirit. He can do great things in your life, and he can minister to you in great ways and use you mightily.

This all comes from understanding him and an understanding of what theology is and the right belief in who he is and who he is meant to be to you.

I hope that this has encouraged you. God bless.

Key 5 — Being Set Apart

What do I think "set apart" means? The fundamental principle underlying the understanding of the word "holiness" is to be "set apart for God." In biblical times, priests went through a process of cleansing and purification in order to minster before the Lord.

The Lord has called us to go through a process to become closer to him. I want to share a few Scriptures with you about being set apart. Some of the disciples wrote about this. 1 John 2:15-17 in the New Living Translation says, *"Do not love this world nor the things it offers you for when you love the world, you do not have to love the Father in you for the world offers us only a craving for physical pleasure, a craving for everything we see, and a pride in our achievements and possessions. These are not from the Father but from this world, and the world is fading away along with everything that people crave. Anyone who does what pleases God will live forever."*

We live in a world that is very sensual and enticing. You don't have to watch television for too long before an advertisement comes on, trying to sell something that they think you need, something that you're missing out on unless you purchase that special item. We are assaulted every day in the modern world with images to look at, items to buy and activities to participate in. God wants us to be a holy people. He wants us to be people who serve him and have his interests in our minds, at the top of our hearts, at the forefront of our emotions and in a special place in our heart. He doesn't want us to be carried away with all of the pleasures of the world. He doesn't want us to be distracted by all of the whims and the fancies of the world. He wants us to be committed to him and devoted to him in everything we say and do.

So many people in the world could be financed by the Christian church. So many missionaries need finances, and the people of God have done great works in foreign nations. They would really benefit from our finances and from our support.

Let's take a look at this verse again. "Do not love the world nor the things it offers you. When you love the world, you do not have the love of the Father in you." We live in a world where people pursue a job that's going to supply them with plenty of money so that they can buy a nice house, a nice car, nice clothes and nice possessions. All of these things are somewhat necessary in people's lives, but it depends on how extreme you are in your spending and on what you're doing.

People who live overseas are happy and joyful even though they might not have much. My brother went to Bali on a surfing trip, and he watched the families in the villages, and they were happy. The fathers were home at 5:00 p.m. with their children as the extended family sat down, chatting and conversing with each other. Everyone seemed content. My brother began thinking that we've been sold a lie in the West as we've been tricked into pursuing possessions and going after more and more and filling up our lives with material things that distract us from the true meaning of life and from what really matters. My brother was amazed that these people were poor, yet they were rich in happiness and rich in favor of the Lord.

One of the keys to intimacy with Jesus is for you not to have idols in your life, for you not to have other things that are more important than him. This is what John is talking about when he refers to "loving the world." We need to walk a fine line between loving possessions and the things of the world that are attractive to us and living a life that is consecrated and given over to the full possession of Jesus Christ.

Jesus doesn't want to compete with your job or with your good clothes. Jesus doesn't want to compete with your new car or with your status among other people. Verse 16 of the same chapter states, "For the world offers only a craving for physical pleasures, a craving for everything we see, and a pride in our achievements and possessions."

Jesus doesn't mind us having personal pride in our achievements and possessions, but many people take it further than that. They build their entire self-esteem around their possessions and their achievements, resulting in an unbalanced life. Jesus doesn't like it when a person feels important because of their possessions and their achievements. Jesus loves it when people focus on him as their main reward and their God. He wants people to fall in love with him and serve him with all of their heart.

When you have Jesus as the center of your life and when you delight in him, you delight in what makes him happy. You delight in what makes his life easier and what accomplishes his will more efficiently. The world and its pleasures shouldn't be the center of your attention, but Jesus and his will should be your focus.

Many people look at this and say, "Well, what do you mean 'a craving for physical pleasures, a craving for everything we see, and a pride in our possessions and achievements?' "

Essentially, many people in the world, even many Christians, don't see any issue with loving the things of the world. Many Christians believe that you can live in this world and serve the lust of the world and pursue everything in the world as if everything is fine and dandy. They believe that there's nothing wrong with being rich or with having all that the world offers. They think that people who disagree with them are the ones who are obviously wrong. Interestingly, John isn't the only one who addresses this. James also has some pretty hard words to say in James 4:2, 3: *"You fight in war yet you do not have because you do not ask. You ask and do not receive because you ask amiss that you may spend it on your pleasures."*

James tells us that to receive from God, we need to ask with right motives and ask for money for the right things — to do things that honor God and serve him. He says that you don't receive because you're often asking so that you can spend it on the pleasures and the things of the world. We have to come to grips with the fact that so many people are building their lives on a rocky foundation. They're building their lives on the possessions of the world and the things of the world — extraordinary houses, expensive cars, and the best fashion clothes that you can wear, spending hundreds of dollars on a dress, fashionable handbags, shoes and accessories. They are focusing on material possessions so that they can impress other people.

Many of our lives are lived outwardly in such a way as to impress others with how we look and what we possess and own. Jesus is not into that. Jesus walked around Palestine and Israel, and when asked for money to pay the temple tax, he had to find Peter to go and catch the fish to get money. This is Jesus, the Messiah, and he's caught at a stage where he didn't have money and had to produce a miracle.

Some people teach that Jesus was rich. When the 5,000 men with their women and children needed food (Matthew 14:13-21), and Jesus ordered the disciples to feed them, the disciples claimed that it would take a year's wages to feed them. If Jesus had a year's wages, he would have bought all of the food for them. However, in order to feed them, he had to perform a miracle — multiply bread and fish.

When we have plenty of money with the ability to buy items, such as medications and other health-related needs, we don't 'officially' need Jesus. In Africa, people are healed of diseases and afflictions more easily than we are in the West because the people in Africa are desperate. They don't have the money or the ability to buy the medications to treat their illnesses, but here in the West, we have an abundance of money and possessions. We don't really need God. We can live a rich lifestyle with many loves and possessions. We don't really need to depend on God in our lives.

Jesus wants us to live a life where we need him. He wants us to live a life where we're dependent on his supply and dependent on his answers to our prayers. He doesn't want us to live a life that's chock full of possessions and material items. James 4:4 states, *"Adulterers and adulteresses, do you not know that friendship with the world is enmity with God. Whoever wants to be a friend of the world makes himself an enemy of God."*

James tells us that there's something wrong with the way that most people live and that they are living in error. He quite clearly says that if you serve the world, then you become an enemy of

God. You have to establish what you are doing. How are you living that might be displeasing to God? What are you doing? What are you spending your money on when you could be saving money and buying things that cost less?

You might dress quite well without having designer brands and fashion labels in your clothing. You can always dress less expensively. You don't have to have the costliest model car. You can survive on a lot less and use that extra money for God's kingdom to help supply others with necessary items while you to store your treasure in heaven where the moths and the rust don't destroy it and the thieves don't break in and steal (Matthew 6:19).

Jesus commanded us to store our riches in heaven. He said that life does not consist of the abundance of our possessions. We live on earth where we hunger after the things of the world — possessions that we assume will make us happy. This is simply not the way to an intimate relationship with Jesus.

An intimate relationship with Jesus is found in doing his will and in doing what makes him happy and gives him pleasure.

We need to look at our lives and see what we're spending our money on. The Apostle John quotes Jesus as follows: *"I know your works, that you are neither cold nor hot. I could wish you were cold or hot. So then, because you are lukewarm, and neither cold nor hot, I will vomit you out of My mouth. Because you say, 'I am rich, have become wealthy, and have need of nothing'—and do not know that you are wretched, miserable, poor, blind, and naked—I counsel you to buy from Me gold refined in the fire, that you may be rich; and white garments, that you may be clothed, that the shame of your nakedness may not be revealed; and anoint your eyes with eye salve, that you may see. As many as I love, I rebuke and chasten. Therefore be zealous and repent. Behold, I stand at the door and knock. If anyone hears My voice and opens the door, I will come in to him and dine with him, and he with Me.* (Revelation 3:15 – 20).

Jesus is saying quite clearly here that he's standing outside the door. Jesus is knocking at the door of your heart, but if you're too busy living life high on the hog, you won't even hear his knock.

We need a change of heart. He's waiting at the door of your heart to be given entrance, to be given permission, to come into your life. He's telling us that saying we have need of nothing because we are rich and wealthy. That's our problem in the West — we have our incomes, and we have our possessions. We possess material things, and we are happy with what we have. Of course, when you're seeking possessions and wealth, you never seem to have enough. Even some of the wealthiest people in the world still hunger after more.

Jesus says that people who feel that they're in need of nothing do not know that they are wretched, miserable, poor, blind and naked. These are pretty harsh statements — wretched, miserable, poor, blind and naked. What does he mean by poor? He means that you're not rich in fellowship. You're not rich in your relationship with Jesus. You're naked — in other words, you're not clothed. You're not presented correctly or dressed in the right clothing. You're exposed before God as someone who is going after things that are worthless, things that don't have eternal value, so you're naked before him.

The passage says that you're blind because you're unaware. You can't see the eternal purposes of God. You can't recognize what's eternal and what's important. You're actually blind to it. The god of this world, through preaching and sometimes even through the Church, has blinded the people of God about what's really necessary and worthwhile and what make life precious in the sight of God.

In my book, "Living for Eternity," I tackle the theme of living a life that has plenty of reward in eternity for the people that serve God. I suggest that you buy that book and read it because I go into some more detail. You cannot live in this world, holding on to lust, possessions, enticements and the attractions of the world while possessing Jesus at the same time.

As James stated, you can't be a friend of the world and a friend of God. You have to choose one and decide if you're going to serve your God and how you're going to spend your money.

You might want to know how I personally manage my money. I use a large portion of my money every two weeks when I am paid my disability pension. I spend that to prepare books and publish them. For instance, it will take money to have the videos typed up that I'm preparing this book from. It will take time for me to go through what was typed up and carefully add what was said to make it more appealing to read. Then, it will take me a significant amount of money to have it professionally edited so that it reads really well.

Next, it will cost money to have a cover designed for the book and to have the book published and produced and made available in print and on Kindle. These are all of the things that I need to do to produce this book that you're reading now. In order to set aside this money, I need to give up other things that I could buy, such as better clothes, entertainment and going out to restaurants.

I make many sacrifices in order to produce the books that I write. I don't write them to affect thousands of people. These books aren't the best or the most popular out there, but I write them to reach an individual person. I write them to reach you, the reader, and to affect your life and change it and to give you something to understand and put into practice so that your life becomes more prosperous and more aligned with the will of God.

In order to spend money on writing books, like I've said, I need to set it aside from places that I could spend it instead and divert it toward producing books. A time will come when my ministry operates with enough money coming in to produce books, but I'll always be spending money on the ministry and related expenses. I won't live an extravagant lifestyle even if my ministry becomes popular, producing a lot of money in support.

Another story from my life happened when Jesus told me that I was to work for him. I was put on a disability pension because of a mental illness, and Jesus told me that he allowed that so that I would work full time for him and do what he tells me to do. A few years into that, I grew bored, and I wanted to earn more money to do more things. I went for a trial at a gas station, and if the trial worked out, then I would have part- or full-time work at this gas station. I was doing the trial, but I grew frustrated, and it wasn't working out well. I told the people that I wasn't able to complete the trial, and I walked out.

I was walking down the road in tears with my hopes of getting a job dashed. Jesus talked to me. "Who asked you to get a job?"

I answered, "I thought it was right to earn more money to do more things."

He replied, "I never asked you to find a job. I told you that you're on a disability pension to serve me. I want you to serve me with your time and do what I tell you. I don't want you at a job. I want you to work full time for me."

That was an example of being set apart.

I'm not here to promote earning an income from the government. You might look at that story and say that wasn't really Jesus speaking to me, but I remember how sad I felt that day and how I tried to do a job that would allow me to have more money. I remember Jesus clearly speaking to me and reminding me that he retired me and that he made it possible for me to have an income without working so that I would serve him and have a life that is dedicated to him and his purposes.

That's one illustration of being set apart for him. As I remember that situation, I think, "Would I pursue another job?" I'd only pursue another job if Jesus clearly told me that it was time to do so. I'm currently working in ministry and giving prophecies. People donate money to me for prophecies, which helps to finance the books that I produce.

I can see this method of provision growing over time and providing more funds for books. So far, it has provided me with money for seven books. I'm really impressed as God is leading me and using me to further his Kingdom.

Another key to being set apart is to choose friends that encourage you and help you in your Christian walk. At the same time, distance yourself from people who are negative influences in your life. Get rid of people in your life that aren't encouraging or worse yet, who distract you from your purpose and who don't have a passion for Jesus or promote a holy walk with him. You need to distance yourself from people who are the wrong influences. You will want to get rid of friends who are gossipers, including those that do the following:

- Constantly complain about ministers
- Cut down people in authority
- Gossip about other people
- Continually argue about doctrine or
- Argue with each other.

Even if you are lonely without them, you should leave these sorts of people and choose to have no friends at all instead of friends that are dragging you into disobeying God and not living a life that is pleasing to him.

God doesn't enjoy gossip. God doesn't like it when you gossip or speak badly about pastors. He doesn't like foolish arguments over doctrine. These are things that are clearly addressed in the Bible, and if you have friends like that, God would rather you watch television and listen to sermons online instead of having friends who participate in that sort of living.

I pray that this has helped you and encouraged you. My book, "Living for Eternity," will address this matter more clearly and discusses how to live a life that is set apart and focused on doing things that will matter in eternity. The book talks about storing up your treasure in heaven and what that looks like. Essentially, one of the keys that we've just discussed to greater intimacy with Jesus is to be set apart. God bless.

Key 6 — Word of God

As Christians, we know that the Word of God is an important part of our life. We should be encouraged to read the Bible, and we should build our lives on what it says. We should not only know the Word of God and understand it but allow it to dwell in our spirit, reside in our hearts and live from it. We should make decisions and live our lives based on what it says.

One of the keys to an intimate relationship with Jesus is having your life built and founded on the Word of God so that you know what it says about living your life with key verses in the Word that you apply daily.

I'm going to take some time to share some verses that I hold dear in the Bible. After you read this chapter, I challenge you to get out a pen and seek out the passages in the Word of God that relate to you most strongly.

I encourage you to not only read the passages but to meditate on them. In particular, you might even want to write down the reasons why those passages are important to you.

The Word of God is alive. The Word of God is living. It's sustenance. It's refreshing. It's beneficial to your life.

We need to understand that the Word of God is something that will benefit us. It's something that will inspire us and encourage us on our journey as we persist with the destiny that God has given us.

I came across this Scripture and felt that it related strongly to me. I claimed that this was a verse for my soul. Isaiah 42:6-9 states, *"I, the Lord, have called You in righteousness, And will hold Your hand; I will keep You and give You as a covenant to the people, As a light to the Gentiles, To open blind eyes, To bring out prisoners from the prison, Those who sit in darkness from the prison house. I am the Lord, that is My name; And My glory I will not give to another, Nor My praise to carved images. Behold, the former things have come to pass, And new things I declare; Before they spring forth I tell you of them."*

We can better understand this Scripture if we go through it line by line. "I, the Lord have called you in righteousness." These verses refer to the life of Jesus, who was called in righteousness. But the Lord God has also called me to be righteous, and he calls me righteous when he looks at me through the lens of his Son.

"I, the Lord have called you in righteousness and will hold your hand." Jesus and the Father have helped me and been with me. Each step of the way, they've encouraged me. They really have held my hand. They really have been leading me through life and encouraging me and holding me up and keeping me going in the process of life.

"I will keep you and give you as a covenant to the people." Jesus has called me to be a writer and a teacher. He's called me to the people. There's no use in writing and publishing books if no one's going to read them. God has called me to specifically write journals, which are healing to your soul and kept in your inner man.

He's called me to write books that reach out to others. He's given me a desire to minister as a special person. Jesus came as a new covenant. I'm not a covenant. But he has purposed me to be a special person in the lives of others.

"As a light to the Gentiles." I am called both to people who are not saved and to Christians. He wants me to minister to unbelievers and to be a witness to them. I often witness to unbelievers through prophetic evangelism and share prophecies with people in the street and minister God's grace and his message to them.

"To open blind eyes." Many people read that literally and think that you're called to pray for blind people so that they can see. However, 'blind eyes' often refers to people who are stuck in thought patterns that are keeping them blind and keeping them restricted in how they live their lives.

Jesus called the Pharisees blind guides. They were leading people, but they were blind to the truth. He's called me to open blind eyes. He's called me to illuminate the truth of the Gospel and the message of the Bible to people.

"To bring out prisoners from the prison, those who sit in darkness from the prison house." For many years, I was bound in sin. God is calling me in the future to write a book to expose the weakness that I have in my life and to give other people an opportunity to understand how I was bound and to read a testimony of how I was freed.

He wants me to do that to help people who are bound in the prison house of addictions so that they can break free of those addictions and know that the truth shall set them free in the power of God. The grace of God can break those bondages.

People sit in the prison house, bound as prisoners, when they believe in religion and in a whole lot of law keeping and understanding of God as angry. I'm called to share the truth of Christ and the message of God to illuminate the correct path and way of believing for people to follow. Through sharing the truth, I'll set people free from their wrong beliefs and their wrong mindsets.

It says, "I, the Lord that is my name. And my glory is not given to another." The Bible holds many promises and prophecies. Many people are declaring that I carry the glory of God and that the glory of God is on me.

The Lord is saying that he's going to give me a share in his glory. He doesn't accept praise given to graven images. "I will not give my glory to another nor my praise to graven images." I feel that people don't really bow down to a graven image anymore, but they do practice idolatry. They do idolize cars, houses and other inanimate objects.

As you can see from the previous chapters, the Lord has directed me to call people out of living for the world and living in the world and to stop practicing the world's pleasures.

"Behold the former things have come to pass and new things I declare. Before they spring forth I tell you of them." The Lord is continually showing me the truth and leading me through prophetic words from other people. He does tell me what is coming to pass in my spirit, and he confirms it in prophetic words that I receive.

This is a foundational Scripture in my life. Many of you can read that verse and claim it yourself if you are called to ministry.

When I look at that passage, I'd say to myself that when Isaiah actually penned that Scripture, he wrote it down for me. He was unaware when he wrote it that he was writing a mission statement for my life.

I was so encouraged to find it and meditate on it. This passage really builds intimacy with Jesus. It showed me my purpose and told me what I'm here for. It keeps me aligned with what I'm meant to do.

Another Scripture that appeals to me and that I'm claiming for both now and in the future is Isaiah 60:1-6:

"Arise, shine; For your light has come! And the glory of the Lord is risen upon you. For behold, the darkness shall cover the earth, And deep darkness the people; But the Lord will arise over you, And His glory will be seen upon you. The Gentiles shall come to your light, And kings to the brightness of your rising. "Lift up your eyes all around, and see:
They all gather together, they come to you; Your sons shall come from afar, And your daughters shall be nursed at your side. Then you shall see and become radiant, And your heart shall swell with joy; Because the abundance of the sea shall be turned to you, The wealth of the Gentiles shall come to you. The multitude of camels shall cover your land, The dromedaries of Midian and Ephah; All those from Sheba shall come;
They shall bring gold and incense, And they shall proclaim the praises of the Lord."

The Lord has promised his people in Isaiah 60 that certain people will carry the presence and the glory of the Lord, and their skin will shine. I've had four or five times in the past where my skin has shone like the sunshine. People have stared and wondered and approached me to ask what it was.

This Scripture says that the glory of the Lord has risen upon you. "The Gentiles shall come to your light and kings to the brightness of your rising." I have had prophecies that said that one day, I'd be called to consult kings and to share revelations, instructions and counsel with leaders of countries. Of course, I don't say this to boast as I have not been called to consult leaders yet, but it has been prophesied over my life a few times.

"Lift up your eyes all around and they shall gather together. They shall come to you. Then you shall see and become radiant." This real imagery shows a picture of people shining, of being able to see the glory on certain people and of those people coming to give of their wealth.

"Because the abundance of the sea shall be turned to you and the wealth of the Gentiles shall come to you." You can reach a certain stage where the glory of the Lord is so present in your life, that people who look for those things and people who are attracted to God will recognize something special in those people as the glory resides on them.

This promise of Scripture is especially dear to me. It keeps me going. I'm walking in a measure of that glory. It's only going to continue and get stronger and stronger as I follow Jesus.

It is so special when you read Scriptures that have been prophesied by true prophets of the Bible that clearly relate to you. I have had, as I have said, a few occasions when people have told me that my skin was shining like the sun. I personally believe that in the future, people will see many others shining, and just like this passage shares, they will seek out those shining ones for prayer and ministry. They will bring their wealth with them to give to those shining ones. More about this can be found in my book, "Optimistic Visions of Revelation," scheduled for release in October 2016.

It is amazing how many times I have read this verse. While it has a corporate meaning for Israel, individuals can also claim and manifest it in their personal lives as well.

Another Scripture that is relevant to me and that leads and directs me is in Jeremiah 1. Most of Jeremiah 1 appeals to me, but verse 10 says, "See, I have this day set you over the nations and over the kingdoms, To root out and to pull down, To destroy and to throw down, To build and to plant."

This verse talks of pulling things down, destroying them, throwing them down and then building and planting. My job as a writer and a prophet is to expose darkness. Expose wrong teachings. Expose wrong doctrines. I am called to expose wrong understandings that people have — beliefs that are keeping them in bondage and keeping them from fulfilling their destiny and God's plan for their life.

Part of my calling is to throw down those things and destroy them in the lives of people. That's similar to Isaiah 42 when it talks about setting people free from the prison house and opening blind eyes. The process is the same — calling out the darkness, exposing the lies in people's lives and sharing the truth for them to follow.

One of the keys that I shared was coming out of the world, separating yourself from it and being set apart. People can easily be trapped in this type of darkness. The world lies and tells you that you can serve the world and God at the same time. People who try to straddle both realms to seek the best of the world and the best of God are lukewarm, according to what Jesus says in Revelation 3. You are neither hot nor cold. Jesus says that people who serve the world are blind, poor, naked and wretched.

In addition, James, the brother of Jesus, also said that if you serve the world, then you're an enemy of God. You must root out and pull down these structures. People have to destroy these strongholds in their lives.

Then, something else has got to take their place. Truth must be preached and shared with people so that they can grow in a productive life, a sustaining life and one that is honorable and pleasing to God.

I'm not just called to point my finger and declare what's wrong. My job is to also provide a replacement of belief and understanding with directions for people to live a prosperous and God-centered life. I want to help them follow God and live as well pleasing to him.

Many people label others — they call people false prophets, speak negatively and point out flaws. But they don't suggest anything better. They're just pulling down.

They are just being critical but not suggesting a better lifestyle or putting out a book on "How to Live the Proper Christian Life." They are just attacking people, doctrine and ideas. That's not the job of a prophet.

Anyone can look at bad theology, bad doctrines, bad teachings and call them out. But the job of the prophet is to pull down the error and restore it with something worthwhile. It's a two-fold job. I base my life on that. I have presented this Scripture in this light.

I hope you understand what I am doing here. All of these Scriptures that I am sharing might not relate to you and to your life, but they are foundational Scriptures to me. You have to search the Bible and find key verses for your life. Then, you need to meditate on those passages and transfer them from head knowledge into your heart so that the Scriptures speak to the core of your spirits. Only when your whole life's purpose is framed by God's Word will you grow into a deeper relationship with Jesus.

Another key Scripture that's very important to me is Romans 8:28: *"And we know that all things work together for good to those who love God, to those who are the called according to His purpose."*

This verse has been very instrumental in my life. I understand that all things work together for good, and that has allowed me to prevail and keep on pursuing God even when things are looking really sad. I persist even though I'm suffering badly and going through a hard time.

Everyone needs revelation on this verse because it will deeply encourage you when you understand it. It means that everything that happens in life, everything that happens to you might not be ordered by God but can be used by him and work out for the good, for a better life and for his glory.

This verse is very special to me and has encouraged me and kept me going many times. I enjoy quoting it to myself and believing in this promise. I know how to persist and pursue the things of God despite the circumstances, making it into a strong testimony and bringing together wonderful stories that encourage and inspire people.

The following verses in 1 Corinthians 1:26-29, also written by Paul, speak to me as well.

> *"For you see your calling, brethren, that not many wise according to the flesh, not many mighty, not many noble, are called. But God has chosen the foolish things of the world to put to shame the wise, and God has chosen the weak things of the world to put to shame the things which are mighty; and the base things of the world and the things which are despised God has chosen, and the things which are not, to bring to nothing the things that are, that no flesh should glory in His presence."*

I've had a mental illness for 20 years. I'm believing for my healing to manifest. A mental illness with mental health struggles makes you appreciate this verse that talks about foolish, weak and base things.

However, this verse really brought healing, comfort and understanding to my life that many wise, according to the flesh, not many mighty, not many noble are called, but God has chosen the weak things of the world to put to shame the wise.

I consider myself one of God's weak vessels whose life is being used powerfully. This foundational Scripture really encourages me.

I base my life on this word that my foolishness might become wisdom to God. The verses say that I can write, encourage and teach people through the leading and understanding of the Holy Spirit and through his inspiration in my life.

Who am I to write and share on the intimacy of Jesus Christ? I don't have a college degree, and I'm not a theologian. I am not wise by man's standards.

However, I can share simply because I have an intimate relationship with Jesus Christ. I'm a writer, and I feel obligated to record a series of videos and have them transcribed and edited by myself. I then send them to my editor to make them into a book that will teach people how to grow intimate with Jesus.

Some people call me foolish. But I'm a fool for Jesus, and this verse is very healing to me. God still uses simple and broken people, people with problems in their lives, to bring him glory and to make his power and his Name well known. God can shine and release his glory through imperfect vessels.

These verses are very poignant and special for me to share, and I base my life on them. I hope they encouraged you. Let me share a couple more Scriptures. This one is integral to how I live my life. Proverbs 3:5-6 tells us, *"Trust in the Lord with all your heart and lean not on your own understanding. In all your ways acknowledge Him and He shall direct your path."*

So many people live their lives and do not trust God and are not led by him. They make decisions based on their mind and on their own understanding instead of trusting the Lord and being led by the Holy Spirit.

Being led by the Holy Spirit is a real process. I often address this topic in my books. I live my life by being led by the Holy Spirit.

The Holy Spirit dictates what I do each day. He leads me to get up and make and produce a video that will become this book. The Holy Spirit led me to write down this verse to share with you.

"In all of your ways acknowledge Him and He shall direct your paths." We are to give glory to God and to say that God is directing us. We are to acknowledge God in all that we do. God then will make sure that he directs our path. He will vindicate us when we are maligned, and he will make our name great and glorify us in front of other people.

The more the Lord glorifies a person, the more he is glorified. The more a person becomes popular because of God, the more God gets the glory for that person's success. Many people are successful due to God's help, but they don't acknowledge him or give him the glory. I refuse to let that happen in my life.

As I write books and as I become more popular, I focus on God. I acknowledge him for leading my life and being part of my life.

I just have one more Scripture to share that many of you know well. One little aspect of the passage means a lot to me: Jeremiah 29:11-13 states, *"For I know the thoughts that I think toward you, says the Lord, thoughts of peace and not of evil, to give you a future and a hope. Then you will call upon Me and go and pray to Me, and I will listen to you. And you will seek Me and find Me, when you search for Me with all your heart."*

Many people know verse 11, "For I know the thoughts that I think toward you, says the Lord, thoughts of peace and not of evil to give you a future and a hope." But they stop reading there. They don't go on to verses 12 and 13 that say, "You will call upon me and go and pray to Me, and I will listen to you. And you will seek Me and find me, when you search for Me with all your heart."

When you search for God with all of your heart and when you apply yourself to the discipline of listening to Jesus, you will find that Jesus and God and the Holy Spirit speak back to you. The only prerequisite to finding them and dialoguing with them is doing it with all of your heart.

If you pursue them with all of your heart, the Word promises that you will find God and that he will be found by you. I love that aspect of that verse. While verse 11 is certainly encouraging, verses 12 and 13 are even more encouraging, which say that if you seek God, he will listen to you. He will hear your prayers and be found by you.

These verses are such an encouragement. I approach God and Jesus with all of my heart and have always heard from them. Whenever I initiate a conversation with them, they always reply. It saddens me that the majority of Christians don't have a two-way relationship with God and Jesus where they can converse. By using the right books as resources that teach you how to hear from God and with the earnest desire to seek God with all your heart, I am sure that you could find success.

I build my life on these encouraging and integral verses. I could have shared other passages as well. You need to have a store house of Scriptures from the Bible upon which you build your life.

Success in the Christian life is properly understood as lived and directed by God and founded on Scripture. It's founded on the eternal truth of an intimate relationship with Jesus and growing with him. You need solid truth in your life with a foundation that will never fail you. That truth is found in the Bible.

Key 7 — Friendships

You need to maintain solid friendships when it comes to God, your relationship with him and intimacy with Jesus. Wholesome friends, people who serve God and delight in him with all of their hearts, will encourage your intimacy and friendship with Jesus.

Friends that are negative influences or that practice and do things that are unacceptable to God will corrupt your behavior. 1 Corinthians 15:33-34 says, *"Do not be deceived: Evil company corrupts good habits. Awake to righteousness, and do not sin; for some do not have the knowledge of God. I speak this to your shame."*

Certain people will lead you into sin. They have sin in their own life, so if you hang around with them or spend time with them, then you'll start to participate in the same sins that they are involved in. You must develop strong and wholesome friendships that edify and please God. You need to avoid spending time with people that can corrupt your good behavior.

My former pastor, Mitchell, who is also my friend, is a wonderful example of Jesus' grace. He's understanding, loving and really is like a little Jesus on earth. He demonstrates the love and compassion of Jesus Christ.

He's human. He's got faults, and he's got things that test him. He has trials and tribulations in his life. But he's open and transparent with them, and he's willing to share them with me and from the pulpit. His vulnerability with me makes him easy to relate to as a friend.

He spends time with me, one on one, and we discuss many things. He is very interested in what goes on in my life. He takes a vested interest in the books that I'm producing and the ministry that I'm participating in. He listens as I share about all aspects of my life and encourages me in those things and builds me up. He always asks me to spend more time with him, so I visit him at the ministry center where he has his church. I need to pay attention to his interests and spend more time with him.

I had another friend, Sarah, for a number of years, who was a pastor's daughter. Her father pastored our church for a time. She was very loving, and she believed in the Gospel of grace, in a God that wasn't angry or a disciplinarian, but a God of love, favor and compassion.

Through her involvement in my life, I was able to come out of the thinking that God is cranky and angry. Sarah gave me books that showed the message and liberty of grace and the understanding of how Jesus really loves us and how he wants us to see ourselves. She not only believed in the grace of God, but she actually proved the grace of God by how she lived her life.

She demonstrated that unbiased and unrelenting grace of God. She was someone who didn't just speak about love but who loved in an extraordinary way. She loved in a way that was overflowing and abundant with meaning and purpose. She loved me even though I was an angry person who was frustrated and stuck in my old covenant understanding of an angry God.

I was a man who believed that he was right all the time, and I couldn't be told that I was wrong. She took the time to get to know me and to listen to my stories. She listened to me for many,

many hours and let me talk and talk and talk while she just sat and asked questions and took the time to love me.

Eventually, she started to challenge some of my beliefs. She began asking me questions about certain issues. Then, she came out and point-blank refused to believe certain things that I said and told me when my beliefs were wrong. When I did more reading and research on what she said, I found out that I agreed with her. Twenty-one times she told me that I was wrong, and 21 times out of 21, I found out that she was right.

Her understanding, compassion, demonstration of love and active engagement in my life gave me the chance to reevaluate what I believed. I reexamined how I was bound and came to understanding that the doctrines that I believed in were wrong. Through her love and compassion for me, I came to find teachings on the Gospel of grace and was finally set free by books like "Destined to Reign" by Joseph Prince (Harrison House, 2007).

I found a loving way to live my life. I found total freedom in my expression. I found happiness. I transformed into a joyful Christian instead of one who was angry and who believed in a judgmental God.

My friendship with Sarah is wonderful example of how strong friendships help you develop a closer and more intimate walk with Jesus. As my beliefs and understanding of God changed, I come to realize that Jesus was the image of the invisible God. He perfectly represented God. I grew to understand that God is a God of love and a God of understanding and compassion.

As my opinions of God changed, so did my intimacy with Jesus. I didn't believe that he had an angry Father anymore, and instead, I believed that my sins were forgiven and covered by the blood of Jesus. I come to draw closer to him in a more meaningful and deeper relationship.

This came about through my relationship with Sarah. She helped me see Jesus from a new perspective. She opened my blind eyes.

I was blind and sitting in the prison house. As I shared in these Scriptures, I was bound up with religion, and she came in to my prison. She listened to me. My eyes were opened as she showed me the knowledge of the truth of the Gospel of grace. She not only shared truth with me, but she demonstrated God's grace to me.

When I was angry and argumentative, she didn't argue with me. When I was hard to live with, she accepted me and was patient with me. She had the compassion and love to understand me and to listen to my struggles.

I talked to her for hours and hours. Hours and hours. She gently reminded me that I was telling her the story for the third time. "I've already heard this story two times." She had the patience to listen to one of my stories twice, but on the third time, she'd stop me.

She completely expressed grace to me. She spent hundreds of hours in relationship with me, caring and loving me. She didn't push her grace message on me but instead, demonstrated that message to me.

Many people on Facebook have come to believe in the Gospel of grace. They push their thoughts, feelings and doctrines on other people in a way where they're speaking in capital letters and shouting at them. They condemn people that are stuck in religion or bound up in legalism. They act rudely, and they really lack grace, love, and compassion in how they share their message.

I aim to be different when I share the Gospel of grace with people. I try to be understanding and loving and develop a relationship with them before I share a message that might be contrary to what they believe.

I have many friendships on Facebook and have grown close to people through posts. I have managed a couple of Facebook groups, including "Open Heavens and Intimacy with Jesus" and "Prophetic Training Group." Through running those groups and interacting with people for years, I've developed friendships with godly and wonderful people who bless my life. They add a certain positive quality to my life.

You want these kinds of people in your life, and you want them to post on your Facebook walls where you can read their comments. All of the posts on your wall should be edifying and build you up and encourage you. You want to be able to read your Facebook wall like a magazine and go from one post to the next without scrolling past many. You will be edified by what your friends say as you spend time reading their words. You can fill your wall with encouraging posts by being discerning with your friends and cutting out those who are abrasive, abusive, follow wrong teachings or demonstrate wrong behavior.

I'm very strict with the people that I communicate with. I'm very vigilant about who I remain friends with. It affects your whole life, including the way that you relate to Jesus. Your Facebook friends can positively influence you instead by encouraging, edifying and speaking life into every situation.

I don't have people on my Facebook wall who are negative or those who have wrong theology. I've have some friends who believe in legalism and are in bondage to a judgmental God. I keep some of them as my friends because I know they've got a good heart, and they're like I was and believe in holiness and righteousness. They're just going about it in the wrong way. I have other friends who believe in the message of grace, grace-filled believers who post encouraging words.

I seem to get rid of people who are too judgmental and who think that God is angry and post things that are disruptive, abusive and cruel on their walls. Some of these people seem to shout their message and to condemn others who don't believe as they do.

I have a mixture of friends — people who believed how I used to believe and those who believe like I believe now. I just become the light in the world. I demonstrate and shine my light to both groups of friends, and I post what I feel is closest to my heart by the Spirit of the Lord. I have close friends on Facebook who are in my groups, and I minster to the people in my groups. These relationships benefit me.

It's better to have no friends in your personal life than to have the wrong friends. I'll say that again. It's better to have no friends in your personal life than to have the wrong friends. I have a calling as a prophet, and many people are attracted to me and draw close to me. Sometimes, the wrong spirit in that person comes to attack me, pull me down and upset me. The spirit of Jezebel just wants to disqualify my voice in the world.

Twenty-three years ago, I married a woman with the spirit of Jezebel, and she deeply affected my life. I really loved her. But when we split up, she was very abusive and cruel and operated in witchcraft against me to make sure that I didn't win my custody case for my son. I had a friend who I was close to who was very spiritual. She met my wife and told me that I was never going to progress as a person or as a Christian if I continued seeing my wife.

She suggested that I stop seeing my son. She watched my behavior every week, and she noticed that I became depressed every couple of weeks, and she wondered why. When she met my wife, she realized that my wife was operating in witchcraft so that I never progressed. I would never fulfill my destiny unless I left my wife behind and stopped seeing my son every two weeks, walking away from that relationship.

I was having a problem with walking away from my son because I loved him. He was part of me, and he gave me a reason and a purpose to live. I was having problems obeying what my friend had said. Then Sharryn, my wife, remarried, and she told me that I couldn't see my son anymore.

I was going to fight for my legal rights to be able to see my son every two weeks. However, Jesus told me to walk away from him and not to fight for him like a piece of used furniture in the marriage dispute but to leave him to my former wife and her new husband to bring up.

Around that time, I remembered that my friend had warned me that it would be best if I didn't spend time with my son every two weeks. Since Jesus told me not to fight for my son, combined with what my friend had said about walking away, I finally listened. I didn't see my son for 16 years, which caused a lot of pain, but once again, I obeyed God.

I did this because Jesus told me to do it. He had a reason for directing me this way. My friend, Chloe, who was a spiritual person, told me that I would be better off if I didn't see my ex-wife.

Some people might read this book and think that you could never do that as a loving father. We've got to remember that Jesus left his own Father for 33 years. He was on earth and communicated with his Father, but he was separated from his Father.

The Father agreed that his Son would leave the perfection of heaven to come down to earth. They were separated from each other. Sometimes, God calls for separation when people aren't good for us. He calls us to separation.

Ever since that time about 21 years ago when I last saw my former wife, she hasn't been able to practice any witchcraft against me. I've developed and started to achieve some things, including writing 17 books now. I am very much encouraged in my life.

Part of having an intimate relationship with Jesus is having friends like Sarah who can demonstrate grace, love and compassion to you. You don't want people like my former wife in your life who are disruptive to you and who cause you to be hurt and spiritually affected.

I had a friend named Yianni. For a long time, we were both rejected people who often felt sad about our circumstances. I used to go out with him, and we spent the whole night talking.

At one time, I had the spirit of Jezebel myself. I spent a lot of time with Yianni, and the Lord told me to stop hanging around him and to break off the friendship. He essentially told me this scripture in 1 Corinthians 15: 33, *"Do not be deceived: 'Evil company corrupts good habits.' "*

Yianni constantly gossiped about others and criticized our leaders. He regularly made negative comments. I later found out from others that whenever he talked about me, he attacked me and shared my secrets and personal information with them. People came to me and asked, "Why do you have Yianni as a friend? He's always speaking negatively about you."

I questioned him about this once. "You always speak negatively to me about everyone that we know. I wonder what you say about me when you're with other people, and I'm not there." He got quiet, which was typical of him as he didn't enjoy confrontations. With sadness, I had to remove him from my life.

At one stage, he was my only friend in life, and it was particularly hard to spend time by myself at home with my TV and with the internet. I struggled to cope without going out and having company, but God called me to do these things. We have to be obedient to Jesus like the first key I shared in this book.

We have to be sure that Jesus knows what he's doing, and when Jesus tells us to do something, we need to listen and obey what he tells us because he's got our best interests at heart. He has our lives in his hands, and he's only got good things for us. He doesn't want us to continue in relationships that hurt us. He wants to change that so that you only spend time with people that are edifying and beneficial.

Of course, you can spend time with the broken hearted and minister to the addicts, heretics and the homeless. God isn't calling you away from those relationships where you minister to others. He just doesn't want you to go out for coffee and spend copious amounts of time with someone who's practicing a lifestyle of sin — gossiping, sinning, speaking negatively or coarsely and demonstrating bad fruit when it comes to the Christian life.

Jesus essentially says that it's better to have no friends than to have bad friends. Some of you need to hear this. Certain people who are reading this book have friends in their lives who distract them from God. Jesus is telling you through this book to break off friendships with these people and even to quote this verse to them, "Do not be deceived: 'Evil company corrupts good habits.'"

Tell them that the Lord has spoken to you that you can't hang around them until they stop doing the hurtful behaviors they're involved in. You can gracefully say that to your friend, but you need to break it off and come apart and be separate for God so that you are not influenced by that person.

I had another friend who was very lonely and so was I. But when I spent time with him, I became angry more often. I'm not really an angry person anymore, but I used to regularly get frustrated and angry in his presence. He mentioned that I was often angry. I told him that it was his company that was doing it to me. I cut off my friendship with him and stopped spending time with him.

I have many friends online. I've got friends at my community center that I can go and visit and spend time with. But I spend most of my time alone with the internet and with God and with

Jesus. I have a tremendous relationship with Jesus. We talk most days and at night as I go to sleep. He leads me and demonstrates his grace and love to me. He shows his compassion in my life, and he is the light of my life. He leads me in everything I do and teaches me.

He's the one who, through the Holy Spirit, gives me the ideas of what to write in my books. The Holy Spirit especially inspires me to do a series of videos or write a book. Jesus walks with me and holds my hand like Isaiah 42 says. "He will hold my hand," and he talks with me, and he gives me joy in the journey.

I pray that this has been an encouraging book for you. You've learned a lot, and I pray that you will go through each of the steps and develop each of the keys that I've mentioned in this book. I pray that you will practice them and apply each of these seven keys in your life. Demonstrate each one so that you become closer to the Lord and so that you have an intimate relationship with Jesus.

Closing thoughts

This book is quite heavy on my testimonies and my life and a little short on discussing each of the keys. I have reviewed and edited the book, and I am happy to leave it as it is. Even so, it might not have been the book that you were looking for.

Thousands of books address these topics, but the authors only really open up with transparency about these subjects in just a few of them. I am quite certain that I have demonstrated each of the keys as I have shared my life with you.

There might be 20 keys to intimacy with Jesus, 13 of which I have not covered in this book. This book was an expansion of a one-hour interview that I did on a radio station. I took the seven keys that I mentioned in that interview and made a 30-minute video on each of them.

You can see that one-hour video here on the Kindle book:

https://www.youtube.com/watch?v=LEhIH4nSQ8A

You can search for the video on YouTube under the title "Intimacy with God (Revealing the Christ in You)" if you are reading the paperback.

I'd love to hear from you

One way that you can bless me as an author is by writing an honest and candid review of my book on Amazon. I always read the reviews of my books, and I would love to hear what you have to say about this one.

Since I read a lot of books, I always make sure to read the reviews of any books before I buy them. You can easily make a good decision about a book when you have read enough honest reviews from readers. One way to make sure this book sells well and to give me positive feedback is to write a review for me. It doesn't cost you a thing but helps me and the future readers of this book enormously.

To sow into my book-writing ministry, read my blog or to request your own personal prophecy from me, you can visit http://personal-prophecy-today.com. All of your gifts will go toward the books that I write and self-publish.

To write to me about this book, please feel free to contact me at my personal email address at survivors.sanctuary@gmail.com.

You can also friend request me at Facebook at Matthew Robert Payne. Please send me a message if we have no friends in common as a lot of scammers friend request me.

You can also do me a huge favor by sharing this book on Facebook as an enjoyable book to read. This will help me and other readers.

How to Sponsor a Book Project

If you have been blessed by this book, you might consider sponsoring a book for me. It normally costs me between fifteen hundred and two thousand dollars or more to produce each book that I write, depending on the length of the book.

If you seek the Holy Spirit about financing a book for me, I know that the Lord would be eternally grateful to you. Consider how much this book has blessed you and then think of hundreds or even thousands of people who would be blessed by a book of mine. As you are probably aware, the vast majority of my books are ninety-nine cents on Kindle, which proves to you that book writing is indeed a ministry for me and not a money- making venture. I would be very happy if you supported me in this.

If you have any questions for me or if you want to know what projects I am currently working on that your money might finance, you can write to me at **survivors.sanctuary@gmail.com** and ask me for more information. I would be pleased to give you more details about my projects. You can sow any amount to my ministry by simply sending me money via the PayPal link at this address: http://personal-prophecy-today.com/support-my-ministry/ You can be sure that your support, no matter the amount, will be used for the publishing of helpful Christian books for people to read.

Other books by Matthew Robert Payne

The Parables of Jesus Made Simple

The Prophetic Supernatural Experience

Prophetic Evangelism Made Simple

Your Identity in Christ

His Redeeming Love- A Memoir

Writing and Self-Publishing Christian Nonfiction

Coping with your Pain and Suffering

Living for Eternity

Jesus Speaking Today

Great Cloud of Witnesses Speak

My Radical Encounters with Angels

Finding Intimacy with Jesus Made Simple

My Radical Encounters with Angels- Book Two

A Beginner's Guide to the Prophetic

Michael Jackson Speaks from Heaven

Conversations with God: Book 1

Coming Soon

Optimistic Visions of Revelation

Influencing Your World for Christ

You can find my published books on my Amazon author page here:

http://tinyurl.com/jq3h893

About the Author

Matthew was raised in a Baptist church and was led to the Lord at the tender age of 8. Matthew has known some pain and darkness in his life, which has helped him develop a close intimacy with Jesus and led him to have a deep compassion and love for all people.

Today, he runs two Facebook groups, "Open Heavens and Intimacy with Jesus" and "Prophetic Training Group." Matthew has a commission by the Lord to raise up prophets and mentor people in the Christian faith. He does this by training people through his groups and writing relevant books on the Christian faith.

God has commissioned him to write 50 books in his life, and he spends his days earning the money to self-publish and writing the books. You can support him in his mission by donating money at http://personal-prophecy-today.com or requesting your own personal prophecy.

It is Matthew's prayer that this book has blessed you, and he hopes it will lead you into a deeper and more relevant relationship with God.